DATE DUE

BRODART, CO.   Cat. No. 23-221

Beyond the Babble

Beyond the Babble

Leadership Communication That Drives Results

Bob Matha and Macy Boehm

Foreword by Marcia Silverman

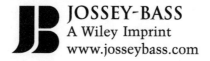

JOSSEY-BASS
A Wiley Imprint
www.josseybass.com

Published by Jossey-Bass
A Wiley Imprint
989 Market Street, San Francisco, CA 94103-1741—www.josseybass.com

Jossey-Bass books and products are available through most bookstores. To contact Jossey-Bass directly call our Customer Care Department within the U.S. at 800-956-7739, outside the U.S. at 317-572-3986, or fax 317-572-4002.

Jossey-Bass also publishes its books in a variety of electronic formats. Some content that appears in print may not be available in electronic books.

Library of Congress Cataloging-in-Publication Data

Matha, Bob.
    Beyond the babble: leadership communication that drives results/Bob Matha and Macy Boehm; foreword by Marcia Silverman.
      p. cm.
    Includes bibliographical references and index.
    ISBN 978-0-470-20048-3 (cloth)
      1. Communication in management. 2. Leadership. I. Boehm, Macy. II. Title.
HD30.3.M378 2008
658.4'5—dc22

                                           2008009382

Printed in the United States of America
FIRST EDITION
HB Printing 10 9 8 7 6 5 4 3 2 1

Contents

Foreword   ix

The Authors   xiii

Acknowledgments   xv

Introduction   1

1. The Power of Communication   9

   On Strategy Communication Cuts Through Babble   14
   Effective Communication Gets Results   16
   Why Communication Makes a Difference   19
   Summary   23

2. On Strategy Communication: An Overview   25

   The Action Equation   27
   The People Channel   34
   Summary   43

3. *Do:* What Do You Need Employees to Do?   45

   The Elements of On Strategy Direction   47
   Setting a Clear Path for the Land of Oz   57
   Summary   61

4. *Know:* What Do Employees Need to Know to Take Action?   63

   They Need to Know Why   64
   Who Needs to Know?   70
   The Land of Oz Knows   74
   Summary   74

5. *Feel:* What Do Employees Need to Feel to Take Action?   77

Be an Organizational Psychologist   82
Getting the Insights You Need   83
The Land of Oz Gets Emotional   84
Summary   85

6. The "Why Nots": What's Getting in the Way?   87

The Behavior Chain   88
Addressing a "Why Not"   92
Be an Organizational Archeologist   95
The Land of Oz Confronts Its Demons   98
Summary   100

7. Package: Turn the Action Equation into a Conversation   101

Conversations Are "In the Moment"   103
The Memory Issue   104
The Conversation Platform   105
The Land of Oz Gets Ready to Roll   108
When Issues Are the Issue   108
Summary   114

8. Align: Make Sure All Leaders Are On Strategy   117

Don't Be Fooled   118
Start at the Top and Work to the Front Line   120
Promote Open Discussion at Multiple Levels   122
Include Informal Leaders in the People Channel   125
Summary   126

9. Equip: Give Leaders the Tools They Need to
Communicate On Strategy   129

Train Leaders as if Strategy Depended on It   130
Support Local Leaders and the People Channel   135
Recognize and Strengthen the Weak Links   139
Complementary Leader Assignments   141
Summary   143

10. Drive and Support: Orchestrate and Sustain On
Strategy Conversation   145

Create a Drumbeat   146
To Raise the Volume, Run a Campaign   154

How Communication (the Function) Can Help   158
Summary   165

11. *You:* The Top Leader's Role   167

Expect a Lot   167
Measurement   169
Reward, Recognize, and Hold Accountable   174
Prioritize   175
Lead by Example   176

12. "How to" Resource Guide   179

Conducting Discussion Groups   179
The Memory Game   186
Alignment Interviews and Snapshot   187
The Consider-Dialogue-Solve Process   191
Conducting a "Red Face" Test   193
Identifying Informal Leaders   195
Selecting Vehicles: Opportunities Abound   196

Glossary of Terms   205

Notes   207

Index   209

Foreword

Communication is the most natural thing in the world. At just a few months, babies show pleasure by laughing and unhappiness by fussing. Most of us are saying simple words at one year of age. The fact is, humans are born to communicate. So why in the world is *real* communication so difficult, especially in the business arena?

That's a question I have asked myself throughout a decades-long career in public relations. In that time, I have worked with dozens of corporate executives, government officials, and entrepreneurs to help them shape their messages and communicate clearly and distinctly to the general public, investors, and employees.

Most of the time, I have succeeded. But if I had had a copy of *Beyond the Babble* throughout my career, I think my success rate with clients would have been 100 percent.

That doesn't surprise me, because I have had the pleasure of knowing and working with Bob Matha and Macy Boehm for a number of years. Bob and Macy have an unexcelled track record as communicators, both in the broader field of public relations and, especially, in workplace communications.

Bob Matha developed the award-winning workplace communications practice *Ogilvy PR Inside* for Ogilvy PR Worldwide (where I serve as CEO) and once headed our Chicago office. He has focused on communications issues surrounding workplace performance for more than twenty years.

Macy Boehm is also an Ogilvy PR alum; she served there as a senior counselor and was coleader, along with her coauthor, of *Ogilvy PR Inside.* Macy has worked from the C-level suites to the front line, primarily for Fortune 150 companies, helping them align their employee communications with their strategic business direction.

Now Bob Matha and Macy Boehm have distilled their wisdom about—and experience in—employee communications to create

Beyond the Babble. This is a book that should be read not just by PR and HR professionals, but by executives at the highest level of any corporation, because it clearly demonstrates that much of what passes for internal communications today is, in fact, babble.

If you have spent enough time in the business world, you will instantly recognize what Matha and Boehm mean by "babble." It's the videos, posters, newsletters, and "vision and values" statements that are churned out by the thousands in corporate America yearly. It's that endless PowerPoint presentation on corporate goals that inspires only the desire for a nap. It's that bulging three-ring binder on strategic objectives that, once produced, lives on the office shelf for a few years until another bulging binder takes its place.

As the authors put it, "Babble is a key reason behind employee antipathy toward management and apathy concerning strategy execution." It's a prime reason why Gallup finds, year after year, that more than 50 percent of U.S. employees are "not engaged" in their work and, even more ominously, some 15 percent are "actively disengaged." Babble results in employees without a sense of direction or meaningful investment in their work—and that is a prescription for disaster in any organization.

So how does an organization get *Beyond the Babble?* Matha and Boehm articulate the concept of On Strategy communication. And when it comes to not babbling, they practice what they preach, saying "On Strategy communication focuses on answering one critical employee question: What do you want me to do? Then it motivates them to act."

As Matha and Boehm point out, answering that question in a way that motivates doesn't require the charisma of a Jack Welch or the public speaking skills of a Bill Clinton. What it does require is ". . . the ability for leaders to have a meaningful conversation with people." And a meaningful conversation isn't about milestones and metrics; it's about telling employees what you want them to do, and why, in as simple and concise a manner as possible.

Early on, the authors tell the story of "the most extreme case of babble" they ever encountered as consultants. It was a direct sales organization for whom tens of thousands of men and women around the globe sold products door-to-door. As you can imagine, this type of sales work requires tremendous self-confidence, so management made it a point to never share any bad news. The authors write that "The company always distributed good news and buried the bad."

The company became so dictatorial that, amazingly, corporate employees were forbidden to even talk about negative things—everyone was expected to be happy, smiling, and a "team player." Of course, this meant critical operational issues went unaddressed and creative problem solving disappeared because, after all, there were no problems. After several years of disappointment in new product development and a failed attempt to alter its distribution system, the company saw sales and earnings trend dramatically downward. Finally, the parent company installed new management, which decided that, first, there had to be a 20-percent reduction in corporate staff. The babble could have easily continued, but the new CEO recognized something had to change and it had to start with the way they talked with employees. You'll learn just what happened in Chapter One, but suffice it to say that cutting the babble was an invaluable step in turning that business around.

Honest communication can bring about great rewards in business. Coauthor Bob Matha learned that early in his career, when he supported Johnson & Johnson in its crisis management effort during the tragic random poisoning of packages of Tylenol in Chicago in 1982. The company's response to this horrific incident forever set a high benchmark for frank, open communication between a company and the public. An event that might have otherwise destroyed a trusted brand instead made that brand a hallmark of integrity.

Fortunately, few CEOs will ever have to confront an internal communications issue that dramatic, but being open and honest—and asking basic, direct questions—can actually do wonders in preserving a company's advantage in the marketplace, or in orchestrating a turnaround. Matha and Boehm tell the story of a heavy manufacturer that had floundered for years, seeing its stock price plunge by 90 percent over a decade. Cost cutting had been continual, consultants came and went, and the organizational structure was constantly fiddled with.

Nothing helped until the CEO made communication an important part of his job description. In addition to bringing top management into the communication process in formal and informal ways, this CEO went to visit employee groups at all levels. He asked them just two questions: What are we doing that makes you feel proud? What could we do better? These weren't just queries to make employees feel "connected." The first question let the CEO take the company's emotional temperature; the second alerted him to business issues.

Within a few years, as new product development rebounded, the company's stock went from $10 a share to $50. As the authors write, "Employees became proud again and focused not on being victims, but on driving results."

Beyond the Babble would be worth reading simply for inspiring anecdotes like the two I have cited. But Matha and Boehm go well beyond storytelling, giving the reader a formula for implementing On Strategy communication in three steps.

Step One is devoted to ensuring that leadership's message is on strategy and compelling. The authors start with the *Action Equation,* which focuses management thinking on "what employees need to *do* in order to execute strategy or support the company's position on an issue." That thinking then expands to ". . . address what employees need to *know* and *feel* so they take the right actions." The Action Equation, then, is Know + Feel = Do.

In Steps Two and Three, designated company leaders prepare for and bring to life a *People Channel,* talking to employees at all levels directly, "to deliver direction, perspective, and information, and to pull feedback up from the ranks." Again, the emphasis is on talking *to* people, not talking *at* them with charts, posters, and faux inspirational slogans.

The beauty of *Beyond the Babble,* from a communicator's perspective, is that Bob Matha and Macy Boehm take a few simple, basic ideas learned from long experience, present them in a straightforward manner, and then show the reader precisely how to implement them. These are ideas that can—and should—be put into practice by any organization, whether a Fortune 50 firm, nonprofit, or family-owned business with twenty employees.

— Marcia Silverman
Chief Executive Officer, Worldwide
Ogilvy Public Relations Worldwide

⟿ The Authors

Bob Matha and Macy Boehm are partners in and cofounders of Basics 3, a leadership communications and employee engagement firm headquartered in Chicago. They also serve as senior internal communication advisors to clients of Ogilvy Public Relations Worldwide. Bob and Macy have worked together for more than fifteen years to develop the philosophy, processes, and techniques outlined in *Beyond the Babble*. They have coauthored a number of white papers, including *Reinventing Internal Communications to Get Business Results,* which was published in *Public Relations: The Complete Guide* (with Joe Marconi, South-Western, 2004), and they have been featured speakers at the Arthur Page Society and the Advanced Learning Institute.

⟿

Bob Matha has thirty years' experience in business communications as a consultant and as a function head in a major corporation. He is a recognized leader in his field for his breakthrough thinking in how to motivate employees and improve the flow of critical information up, down, and across organizations. Bob began focusing on workplace performance in the mid-1980s while at Premark International, a spin-off from Kraft, Inc. His role included developing and communicating the company's corporate vision, defining and articulating roles and responsibilities between corporate and operating staffs, engaging the organization during a lengthy turnaround period, and integrating several acquisitions. Following his work at Premark, Bob launched an award-winning workplace communications practice at Ogilvy Public Relations Worldwide, a top-ten global public relations firm, served on the firm's management committee, and managed the Chicago office. Earlier in his career, Bob focused on investor relations and crisis management, which included handling communications for Jewel Foods after some forty thousand customers were poisoned with tainted milk, and supporting Johnson & Johnson in its first crisis involving poisoned Tylenol. Bob graduated from Northern Illinois University with a degree in journalism.

—⁓—

Macy Boehm has worked from the CEO suite to the front line. Her primary focus has been to help leaders drive employee behaviors in support of company strategies. Working with Fortune 150 companies, she has helped executive leaders engage employees to deliver new sales strategies, facilitate major changes in compensation and organizational structure, and respond to media and regulatory attacks. For several years Macy led a cross-functional team at a major manufacturing company, served as advisor to the president of the company's largest division, and counseled the CEO on leadership activities. Her work focused on aligning the company's sixteen thousand employees behind its vision and driving successful execution of cost, quality, brand, and union-relationship strategies. Macy also was a senior counselor and coleader at Ogilvy Public Relations Worldwide. At the outset of her career, Macy served as a Governor's Fellow under Indiana's Governor Evan Bayh, who selected her to participate in a leadership development program designed to develop future leaders in state government. She has a bachelor of arts degree in government from Smith College and studied at the University of Edinburgh in Scotland.

Acknowledgments

We want to acknowledge the many clients with whom we've worked over the past twenty years. They face daunting challenges, and we've been fortunate to be able to contribute to their success. Their intelligence, hard work, and dedication to achieving great things make our work, and this book, possible. We also want to acknowledge Kristi Posival and Mike Matha for their work in editing and producing *Beyond the Babble.*

Introduction

A senior executive we know was trying to turn his business around. He knew communication was important to getting this done, and he was very confident in his leadership approach. He developed a vision, mission, values, priorities, and at least three pages of integrated metrics; he held multiple meetings with his management group to review them; and he repeated his message as often as possible. But he felt like he was slogging through mud. "They just don't get it," he kept telling us.

His frustration came to a peak in an off-site meeting. In the middle of a discussion among several of his direct reports, he climbed up on his chair and said, "I don't think you all are hearing me." He went on to repeat his message, this time more loudly. If he'd had a megaphone, he would have used it. The managers looked on with mouths gaping and nodded in agreement. "We hear you," they said. "We hear you." But they still didn't get it.

Many business leaders—especially those at the top of the mountain—believe communication comes to them naturally. They figure they must be good communicators because they are very smart, hold positions of responsibility, and everybody nods when they talk. We deny none of this, but we have news for you. Just because leaders are smart doesn't mean they communicate well. Greater responsibility in finance, or engineering, or project management, or any other business discipline doesn't automatically translate into like abilities in communication (remember, Michael Jordan's ill-fated foray into baseball showed that though he could hit a jump shot, he could not hit a curve ball—so even the greatest talent in one area doesn't always translate to others). Moreover, just because a leader sounds good and has an impressive looking presentation doesn't mean he or she communicates well. In the end, it's not what you *say*, but what your audience *hears*—and, we argue, what your audience *does*—that counts. And the way employees nod at every word? It's often a Pavlovian response to power or, even more likely, a fight against the urge to nap.

The fact is, communicating well is one of the most difficult challenges business leaders face—especially as they get closer to the peak of power. It's also hard for leaders to admit they have difficulties with communicating—and to address those difficulties. They often believe that what worked in their last job will work in a new one, despite an increase in responsibility, risk, and reach. Egos get in the way, along with the inherent complexity of business and the often overwhelming demands on an average employee's time and attention. We've written this book to help leaders learn how to use an important strategic tool—communication—to lead their organizations and get results. It's for management people at all levels, and for staff professionals in communications and human resources who help leaders in their organizations lead. Much of the material may appear targeted to the senior levels of an organization, but anybody who leads a group of people can benefit. If your organization is like most—in which employees don't understand strategy, participation is a minority endeavor, and improving communication often means barking more orders, writing more memos, and making more speeches to disengaged (and nodding) employees—then read on. On the other hand, if you lead a sophisticated, knowledge-based organization—in which nearly all employees understand and embrace strategy, communication is a dialogue, participation among all employees is dynamic, and you're getting the results you need—you probably should consider writing a book yourself.

We call the principles we've outlined here On Strategy communication. Although "On Strategy" isn't a particularly euphonious name, it's simple and clear—two essential characteristics of effective communication within an organization. On Strategy is a philosophy of internal communication that gets leaders, managers, supervisors, and employees focused on understanding and delivering strategy. That's what we believe internal communication should be about (if it isn't about strategy—doing the work of the business—why would a business leader focus on it?).

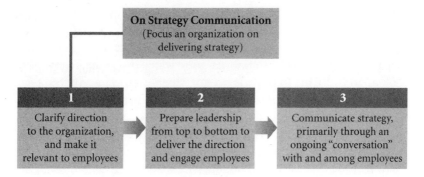

Figure I.1. On Strategy Steps.

On Strategy communication involves three steps, shown in Figure I.1.

The On Strategy approach doesn't deal with external communication, or the communication required simply to inform people of policies, benefits, news, and the like (although we contend that these communications should be strategic as well). It's not "feel-good" communication dealing with "warm and fuzzy" emotions (although managers and employees we have worked with over the years have felt better about their work when communication improves). It's about getting business results through communication. We know that's what business leaders need more than anything else.

The On Strategy approach goes well beyond what most people view as "communications." Much of it lives in the white space between human resources, operating management, executive leadership, and strategy development. One of the problems of living in a white space is that nobody claims it until somebody else starts doing it. We've managed to get around that problem by keeping focused on business objectives and giving the most credit to the people who deserve it—the leaders who actually make things happen.

At the same time, On Strategy communication isn't the "be all and end all" of organizational effectiveness. Organizational development strategies—"big fixes" such as culture change, information flow, organizational redesign, leadership development, knowledge management, and frontline empowerment initiatives—provide long-term benefits that will go beyond the initial benefits of On Strategy communication. We've found, however, that many organizations are not in a position to successfully undertake these types of big fixes without a sound foundation of leadership communication. The On Strategy approach provides that foundation. At the same time, On Strategy communication delivers results quickly, whereas the big fixes take time. For example, the culture change initiatives with which we've been involved took up to two years to provide bottom-line benefits. The On Strategy communication surrounding them delivered results within months, while also contributing to executing the big fixes.

Moreover, the On Strategy approach works with leaders as they are now, not as what one would hope they might be tomorrow. Face it: it's unrealistic to expect a command-style manager to become Dr. Phil overnight, even if he or she takes leadership development seriously. Leaders need tools and a process to start their transformation—tools and process that the On Strategy approach provides. Moreover, they need help getting their jobs done—getting results—while they evolve as leaders. On Strategy communication helps them do that as well.

We've helped leaders apply the principles of On Strategy communication to a variety of organizations—from companies with a hundred thousand employees, to operations with five thousand employees, to groups with six hundred or even just fifty employees. Almost all the work involves profit-making enterprise, although the principles apply just as well to not-for-profits. We hope someday to apply our skills to help schools, youth organizations, and governments communicate better too.

We occasionally include various points of communication theory in the text, but we try to keep those to a minimum. Our purpose here is not to wax philosophical about organizational communications but rather to provide leaders with concrete actions they can take to drive results, and to convince them that these actions will work and are worth the effort. We've left out discussions of how confirmation bias blocks productive interpretation of new information, or how social networks affect knowledge creation and sharing, or how the holographic paradigm can affect communication—among other theories. These might whet the appetite of the academic, but line managers needing results find them tedious. Instead, we've focused on practical ways, relevant to most organizations, to drive employee behavior to get results—and to prepare for, and help deliver, large-scale organizational transformation.

That said, we recognize that some aspects of On Strategy communication are detailed and can be a bit overwhelming, so we have structured the book to make it as accessible as possible. *Beyond the*

Babble is organized in eleven chapters that first explain what On Strategy communication is and why it's important, and then detail how to accomplish the three steps shown in Figure I.1.

Each chapter concludes with a summary, so that busy leaders can jump around in the book and draw on information that is most relevant to them. We have also included a final "How to" resource chapter that reviews some of the key processes we suggest, as well as a glossary of terms (some of which we've created).

In Chapters One and Two, we first review the impact communication can have on business results, then summarize the On Strategy processes. We believe communication has an impact on par with other management disciplines such as strategy development, process management, and human resources. The facts support that contention.

Chapters Three through Seven detail how to clarify the direction leaders provide to an organization and how to make it relevant to employees. This includes a process to distill lengthy business plans—as well as the visions, values, themes, and other attempts at leadership communication—into simple, clear, motivational messages that work. The output enables leaders from the CEO to frontline supervisors to explain strategy in many settings—be they a five-minute elevator ride or a three-day conference about strategy.

Chapters Eight and Nine review how to prepare leaders to communicate to the organization. This includes ways to identify and resolve leadership alignment issues so employees receive a consistent message from different managers across organizational silos. We also review ways to train line managers to become effective in communicating about strategy as well as engaging employees in conversation about strategy.

Chapters Ten and Eleven show leaders how to orchestrate communication in the organization. We review the communication vehicles leaders have at their disposal, the events they can use to trigger strategy communication, how to design a communication campaign around strategy, and the role the communications department can play in On Strategy communication. We also establish the top leader's role in communication.

We've personally worked on every case we mention in the book, except those mentioned by name from the public record, such as Ford Motor Company, BP, General Motors, Home Depot, and NASA. The results achieved in the cases are real. We have left out company names and changed some details to ensure confidentiality, and we have fiddled with timelines and the sequence of events to make it easier for readers to digest the material, but each example is based in fact. When we quote people, the words are theirs, as we recollect them, not ours.

We find considerable intrinsic motivation in doing this work (beyond the obvious need to make a living). We have the opportunity to make a difference in people's lives by reducing the confusion, frustration, tension, and mistrust often found in the workplace. We make life better for leaders by making them more effective—helping them get results. And we help employees see the meaning in their work beyond a paycheck, which makes their work a lot more fulfilling.

Our commitment to this work—and the philosophy outlined in this book—was sealed at a manufacturing plant in the middle of Pennsylvania. We remember first walking through the employee entrance: the grit on the cement floor, the smell of oil used to lubricate the equipment, and the clanking sounds of metal. We heard few sounds of people, though, and it felt cold. We were used to office buildings where, even in hushed tones, people interacted, treating each other with respect, if not warmth. There was none of that here.

It was as if we had walked into a Dickens novel. Men and women toiled on an assembly line, without energy, but with a robotic monotony that seemed almost inhuman. Most of the work was repetitive tasks—the kind that numbs the mind in the best of conditions. They were just going through the motions. Nobody smiled. None of the workers talked to each other. As we walked by, in our suits and shined shoes, they looked at us with contempt. When we approached people on the line to ask a question, they reluctantly paused to answer— even if they were just reading the newspaper. We didn't have that much experience in manufacturing plants, but we knew this was not a very good place to work. Sure, it was safe. The pay was good. People could get as much overtime as they wanted. The union protected the jobs, so there was security. But the environment sucked the energy out of people in just a few minutes.

We felt for the people who worked there—the people on the line, the supervisors, and the management. We knew the plant manager. He was a fine young man, intelligent and energetic. He was very kind. You could see it in his eyes and in the genuine, boyish smile that spread across his face when he forgot where he was. He had a wife and kids and lived in the same town as everybody else. The first day we met him, he told us about how his employees had slashed the tires on his car during the last union negotiation. "I couldn't believe they would do that. These people work here, but they are my neighbors too."

We were able to make a difference in the lives of the people who worked at that plant, because we did our job well: helping people communicate with each other and getting results. We helped them understand each other better, put issues on the table and discuss them, and resolve problems. We helped make the work people did meaningful, so they felt good about it. The last time we visited the plant, it still smelled of oil, and metal still clanked. But the grit was gone. People talked with energy over the production noise. And although we still wore suits and shiny shoes, people from around the plant came up to us and shook our hands, told us about what they were up to, and said it was good seeing us again.

We've been fortunate to have quite a few of this kind of experience. We've always empathized with leaders who face so many daunting challenges, and we believe it is a shame that far too often they are unable to use one of the most powerful tools available—communication—to its utmost potential. With this book, we hope leaders will be inspired to rediscover the power of communication from a whole new perspective and, with that insight, get the results they need and at the same time make the work life of their employees better.

CHAPTER ONE

The Power of Communication

B abble is big in business today. It's the tendency for executives to talk about important issues in convoluted, evasive, or empty terms, and it's evident every day in the newspapers and on television. However, it's much more insidious inside companies than outside them. It corrodes an organization's ability to achieve results, derailing leader and employee alike.

Babble is the PowerPoint presentation filled with lists of priorities, confusing diagrams, and tables full of numbers. It's the multitude of devices leadership trot out to drive action—the visions and values, goals and objectives, metrics and performance indicators, initiatives and priorities. Babble is the clever but empty phrases written to make strategy exciting, and the catchy but irrelevant slogans promoted to build morale and fire up the troops. It's the town hall meetings in which leaders babble through prepared scripts that numb readers and listeners. It's the videos, posters, newsletters, and intranets filled with corporate buzz. In most organizations, there is enough babble to fill a shelf full of three-ring binders. Those binders seldom get off the shelf, and the strategic direction in them gathers dust.

Babble is a key reason behind employee antipathy toward management and apathy about strategy execution. More than half of employees in the United States are "not engaged" in their work, according to Gallup Research. They take a wait-and-see attitude toward their jobs, and results suffer. Even more detrimental to performance is the approximately 15 percent of employees who are "actively disengaged."

According to Gallup, "These employees aren't just unhappy at work; they're busy acting out their unhappiness. Every day, these workers undermine what their engaged coworkers accomplish."[1] According to Gallup's Curt Coffman, a key problem is a lack of clear communication from leadership.[2]

The most extreme case of babble we've encountered was also one of the first we addressed as leadership consultants. That was nearly twenty years ago. It concerned a direct-sales company where every word leadership spoke was positive and every communication, hyperbole. Everything was always "fantastic."

There was history behind the babble. As a direct-sales organization, leaders continually needed to energize tens of thousands of men and women around the globe to sell product door-to-door. The company's performance depended greatly on their state of mind. If anything spooked them—anything—sales would plummet. A rumor spread that a new product was going to be late; sales went down. The company reported lower earnings; sales went down further. There was a heat wave in Europe, and sales went down again.

So management bent over backward to avoid communicating any bad news. The company always hyped good news and buried the bad. Internally, stories of success and achievement filled the company's newsletters and reports, but everyone knew the grapevine was the real source of reliable information (and according to the grapevine, everything wasn't always fantastic). Leadership tried to stamp that out as well, by putting a gag order on its entire employee population. It got to the point where employees were first discouraged, then prohibited, from talking about negative things—even in meetings called to discuss performance.

Babble obscures critical issues from management and employees alike. Results suffer.

The CEO expected everybody to have a "positive attitude." If you raised negative views, you were not a team player—and if you kept it up you were off the team, permanently.

Eventually, all of this babble affected results more than the marketplace, the economy, or competitors. Management left serious issues unaddressed, and the organization's creativity was stifled by the lack of real dialogue. The company experienced continuous failures in new product development and marketing and in its efforts to revitalize its tired distribution approach. Sales and earnings steadily declined over a number of years. Finally, the company's parent replaced top management, and they decided things had to change—starting with a 20-percent reduction in the corporate staff.

For this company, which never talked about anything negative, it was the mother of bad news, and the new CEO knew exactly what he had to do. "We had to turn the company around," he said, "and that started with everybody understanding how bad things were, and how we were going to get out of the mess."

The CEO brought together the company's six hundred corporate employees in a large auditorium, stood alone on a stage in front of them, and explained the situation. He used just a few slides to show some numbers, and he had no notes. He was an average public speaker—nobody would have mistaken him for Winston Churchill. But he told employees the truth, and explained in simple, concise terms where the company was heading and why. He told them they had to reduce costs, and to do so they had to reduce staff. He said they would be working together differently; that all employees needed to surface issues, discuss them, and take action. He outlined a process they would use to reprioritize work, understanding that with 20 percent less staff the organization could not continue to perform as it had in the past. He painted a new picture of the future, saying they would revitalize the company and make it strong again—a vibrant, exciting place to work where leadership valued honesty, creativity, and teamwork. At the end of the presentation, after he answered the last question, employees stood and applauded. For the employees, the prospect of tackling the problems they saw every day was not only a relief, but also energizing.

We encountered babble of a different sort at a major consumer products company, where a senior executive approached us following cutbacks and a reorganization. "We need some morale-building programs to help employees through this," she said. "People are depressed because they don't trust management's judgment, and they are task saturated." We asked what "task saturated" meant, and learned it's a term for when people have too much to do. We asked why people don't trust management, and learned that employees believed management was out of touch with the real issues facing them and the business (just as you would expect of managers who use terms like "task saturated").

Some of the leadership communication approaches she was considering were monthly talks by a counselor about work-life balance, celebrations about achieving big goals, and a poster campaign recognizing high-performing employees. This was babble.

The executive wanted to put some counterproductive Band-Aids on very deep wounds. They would have created less trust in management, not more, because the proposed solutions to the problems were divorced from the reality employees faced. And they would have exacerbated "task saturation" as employees attended meaningless meetings while work piled up on their desks.

Leaders who babble often lose the trust and respect of employees.

Effective leadership communication could, however, address the root of the problem. Leaders needed to explain to employees that they understood their difficulties, then outline processes to overcome them. These could have included ways to reprioritize work to eliminate nonessential tasks, cross-functional collaboration designed to remove time-consuming obstacles, and processes to improve team communication (which saves time and reduces stress). By distracting leadership from real issues with babble around "morale," the executive was doing the employees and her company a disservice.

Babble doesn't make problems go away; it makes them worse. It doesn't hide problems from employees, because employees live the problems every day. It doesn't help people understand reality; it confuses them. It doesn't make leaders look competent or confident; it makes them look unrealistic and out of touch. It does nothing but confuse, misdirect, and discourage.

Babble isn't a challenge just for senior executives. Functional leaders, middle managers, team leaders, frontline supervisors—anybody who needs to lead people to get things done can be sidelined by babble.

And babble affects every employee on the receiving end—the people who ultimately do the work to execute strategy. Consider Greg, a veteran hourly worker in a manufacturing plant. He's union to the bone, and would be our first pick in a bar fight. We first met him years ago when his plant manager asked us to help improve communication.

Babble in the plant came from conflicting metrics and from differences between what management said and what they did.

For example, the plant tracked performance by counting the number of products that came off the assembly line; there was a celebration when they hit record numbers. It didn't matter that the products

> *Babble is a habit that affects senior leaders, managers, and frontline supervisors alike. All must fight it.*

were of poor quality and many didn't work at all—management still posted the rising volume numbers as *the* measure of success. Meanwhile, management talked on and on about quality and customer satisfaction. It was on posters and in the company newsletter. When the company's CEO visited the plant, he told employees in a speech that "our first commitment is to our customers." But that was all babble. Cost and volume production were the only priorities stressed by leadership actions. First time quality ("building it right the first time") dropped as low as 12 percent as management made layoffs to hit cost targets. A faulty product that took too long to fix might sit for months, while a customer waited for it, because employees had to hit volume numbers. In time, the plant became one of the worst-performing operations in the company. For employees, this was a slap in the face. They wanted to be proud of their plant and the products they built, and they resented management for screwing it all up.

Over a two-year period, with our help, the plant manager, Jack, transformed the operation. Jack had been at the plant for a number of years, and it was the only place he'd worked. As a result, he was a product of a culture of "command-and-control" management, and initially did not embrace open communication as an effective leadership tool. New employee research conducted at his operation, however, showed causal connections between communication and operating metrics. Also, several pilot communication programs at his plant showed that a new approach to communication improved results. As a result, Jack changed his thinking about communication and embraced it as a powerful leadership tool. And he had the character, vision, and passion to change how people communicated throughout the plant.

He stopped the babble and started listening to employees. He implemented new communication processes that tapped the knowledge of people up and down the line, management and hourly alike.

They had an ongoing conversation—as an organization—on how to improve performance. He learned that employees were proud of the products they built, but angry with management because quality was so bad. They listened to him as he outlined, in simple, straightforward terms, management's plans (which included significant contributions from supervisors and line employees).

Two years after these efforts took hold, we had the opportunity to visit the plant again. The plant manager asked Greg to tell us what he was up to, and he was very candid. "See this list of jobs?" he asked in a commanding way, and pointed to a quarter-inch stack of papers with lists printed on them. "These are the jobs we used to screw up all the time. It's my job to work with the departments so they don't screw them up any more. See the green marks through the lines? Those are the ones we've fixed. We don't make those mistakes any more. That's what my department used to do—fix those mistakes. We used to have 220 people in my department. Now we have six. I'm almost through with the list."

Then he made a comment that we'll never forget, one that speaks to the power of effective leadership communication: "When the list is done, I'll have to take a new job in the plant. I'm not sure what that will be. I know I won't be making the money I used to. Last year I made more than $100,000. This year I'll make less because we don't have the overtime we did. But we're finally doing the job right." Then he looked the plant manager in the eye and said, "We'll never go back to the way it was. Right?" He was making a statement, not asking a question. When work has meaning to people—when it's more than a paycheck—they take it very seriously.

When Greg was able to cut through the babble, his work was meaningful to him again. He understood what he had to do to build a good product, and he was proud of the product he built. He wouldn't have it any other way. When you embrace real leadership communication as a fundamental business practice, and see the results it can deliver, you won't have it any other way either.

ON STRATEGY COMMUNICATION CUTS THROUGH BABBLE

On Strategy is our term for effective leadership communication. It explains where the company is headed and how it will get there, what employees need to do to make it happen, and why it's important to the business and to them. It's about the business and the realities that affect it. In short, it's On Strategy. More than that, On Strategy communication frames complex business direction in simple, straightforward, motivational terms, so everybody, from the CEO to frontline supervisors, can understand and discuss it. As a result, On Strategy communication makes strategy the topic of conversation in an organization, as employees and managers alike engage in an ongoing conversation about how to execute plans to achieve common goals.

On Strategy communication isn't a speech, a town hall meeting, videos, publications, or pages on the intranet, although these can be useful. The heart of On Strategy communication is in leaders and employees talking to each other—every day—about strategic information and perspective that help them do their jobs and do them well. It depends on not

> *The On Strategy approach is the babble antidote. It frames complex business communication in simple, straightforward, motivational terms.*

only senior executives, but also leaders up and down management ranks—including frontline supervisors. Local leaders are critical because they have continuous and direct interaction with employees. They also are the people best equipped to translate strategy into actionable terms for employees.

Indeed, the managers and supervisors up and down an organization are the single most important communication channel available to any leader or organization. CEOs make speeches, and organizations spend millions of dollars on fancy communication vehicles, but a manager or supervisor can confirm or nullify all these efforts through a single conversation around the water cooler. That's why even frontline supervisors must not only be on board, but also be active in delivering strategic communication. Therefore, when we say leadership, we mean it in the largest sense. Leaders are people who have followers. That might be the CEO, frontline supervisors, or Greg, the hourly worker who led his coworkers to improve quality across their manufacturing plant.

Moreover, On Strategy communication isn't about charisma and style, or refined public speaking skills or showmanship. It does require leaders up and down the organization to be able to have a meaningful conversation with people. In our experience, that's not too much to ask. People have good conversations all the time with their families, friends, and neighbors. They conduct complex business transactions through conversations every day. They buy and sell houses, contract for services, run school boards and churches—the list is long and diverse. They can have effective conversations on strategy as well. They just need the right tools to do so.

On Strategy communication thrives on simplicity. People focus well on a handful of priorities, but they lose their way if the list is too long. When faced with the compendium of visions, missions, values, strategies, priorities, goals, objectives, metrics, and milestones that many business plans throw at them, employees often just shut down. On Strategy communication focuses on answering one critical employee question: What do you want me to do? Then it motivates them to act.

On Strategy communication is emotional. People talk about—and execute—what they care about. Employees in every organization—from a seventeen-year-old kid flipping burgers to a nurse helping terminally ill patients—have some sort of motivational connection to their work. Good leaders tap that connection to drive action. It's what gives work a special meaning. That meaning goes well beyond the rewards and recognition factors to which many leaders limit their focus, and it extends to the intrinsic self-motivations that make people tick. Indeed, these are the most powerful motivators a leader can leverage.

The On Strategy approach requires leadership commitment, process, and discipline. Leaders should no more leave communication to chance than they do strategy development, finance, or process improvement. Moreover, the On Strategy approach is a specific leadership activity. The communication and human resources departments can help orchestrate leadership communication, but the ultimate accountability lies with the leaders themselves. And it's well worth the effort.

EFFECTIVE COMMUNICATION GETS RESULTS

Communication is as effective a tool in improving performance as many of the other disciplines on which leaders spend time and resources. In 2004, in conjunction with the research firm Employee Motivation & Performance Assessment, Inc. (EMPA), we conducted research of twenty-seven major companies, including IBM Global

Services, General Motors, Prudential Financial, Navistar, and other major U.S. corporations.[3] The research identified five communication profiles among the companies: Open, Command, Rumor, Reporting, and Discussion. These profiles were then combined with norms from the National Benchmark Study (run by EMPA in collaboration with the University of Michigan) so that we could measure the impact of employee motivation on business performance over time. Without exception, companies where communication is defined as Open outperform others in key performance categories including growth, profit, and stock prices, as indicated in Table 1.1. Moreover, the correlations indicate that communication is a meaningful driver of that performance. In short, companies that communicate well perform better, and companies perform better because they communicate well.

Profile	Positive Results Correlations	Negative Results Correlations
Open—Information moves up, down, and across the organization in a very fluid, open, inclusive, disciplined fashion	3-, 5-, 10-year stock returns Sales EBITDA IACS Profit margins ROA ROE	None
Command—Information moves from the top down in a tell-and-respond style	5- to 10-year stock returns	Profit margins ROA ROE IACS
Rumor—Information moves from peer to peer as they try to anticipate what the boss wants	Sales EBITDA	3-year stock return
Reporting—Information moves up, as employees cater to the boss	1-, 5-, 10-year stock returns	None
Discussion—People continually discuss, and discuss, and discuss information	3-year stock return	None

Table 1.1. **Impact of Communication on Financial Results.**

Note: IACS = income available for common shareholders.

In the highest-performing companies, communication is open, candid, and flowing. It's as if people in the organization say to each other, "Talk to me, I'm listening." With that kind of attitude toward communication, there is no need for babble. People share, and they keep their focus on strategy.

Contrast this with each of the four other profiles and it's clear that communication makes a difference. Companies with Command communication profiles perform the worst as a group. In these organizations, it's as if leaders say to employees, "Do this and don't ask why. It's none of your business." Employees don't ask why, there is little communication on strategy, and their companies don't perform at peak levels. Companies exhibiting the Rumor profile—in which employees depend largely on the peer-to-peer grapevine—perform better than Command companies, but well behind Open profile companies. The same is true for the last two profiles, Reporting and Discussion, which are troubled by a lack of communication down organizational ranks or efficiency in delivering and considering information.

The research matches our experience. Throughout this book, we will demonstrate the impact effective leadership communication can have on results in case after case. Consider the following:

- A division president of an equipment manufacturer used communication to win support for a new supply chain strategy and process. Historically, functional managers resisted integration because they had to sublimate their local objectives to the interests of the overall supply chain. Leadership overcame these hurdles, however, through use of a cross-functional communication approach, and the company saved millions.

- A plant manager of a 4,500-employee manufacturing operation used communication to turn his plant from one of the worst-performing operations in his company to the best. Communication helped improve first time quality from less than 15 percent to more than 85 percent, achieving record delivery credibility and exceeding cost-reduction targets by more than 150 percent. The plant manager, who became vice president of manufacturing, said of the operation: "We made this plant the diamond of our organization, and it all started with communication."

- A vice president of engineering jump-started innovation in new product development with communication. He refocused and reenergized his staff, and they developed a breakthrough product design that wowed customers and captured market share within weeks of its introduction.

- The executive team of a major airline used communication to win employee support for a controversial acquisition of another airline. Resistance stemmed from seniority issues that put the acquiring airline's employees at a severe disadvantage. After intensive leadership communication, however, employee mindsets shifted.

- A vice president of labor turned the tide of a unionization drive at one of its major operations with effective communication. Facing difficult odds, top leadership communicated to employees primarily through frontline supervisors and won the vote by a 3-to-1 margin. The same company won employee support at another operation for controversial changes to their union contract. Employees, local bargaining representatives, and international union officials first rejected the company's position. With effective communication, however, leadership convinced employees and their union that the changes were essential to make the plant more productive and economically viable, making jobs safer.

WHY COMMUNICATION MAKES A DIFFERENCE

Right about now, you may be saying that communication can't do all that—and in some respects you would be right. Communication is one of a number of performance drivers. Good performance begins, obviously, with an effective strategy (communication doesn't make a seriously flawed strategy brilliant, though it may make it sound a lot better). Good performance also requires smart leaders, resources, hard work, and luck. Communication optimizes all of these (except, perhaps, luck—we're not really sure how that works). Indeed, good communication drives improvement in strategy itself, as employees deeper in the organization contribute their thinking. It makes leaders smarter as communication provides them with more information on which to base decisions. It stretches resources further because it reduces waste caused by actions and energy expended on nonstrategic activities. And it makes hard work pay off, as communication begets results.

At the end of the day, strategy is only as good as its implementation. In fact, many good business leaders ascribe to the axiom "I'd rather have a mediocre strategy well implemented than a great strategy poorly implemented." Great strategy that never is implemented is worthless. Moreover, even the best strategies require midstream corrections, and unless the organization can "change the wheel while you're driving the truck," the strategy won't deliver on its full promise. Communication translates strategic planning into action. Moreover, it engages employees in the organization to make strategy work, so you keep driving on the road to results and not over a cliff.

Communication plays a powerful role in the success of an organization at many levels.

Communication is the face of leadership. Leadership and communication are one and the same. This doesn't mean good communication alone can make a lousy leader great. Moving a large organization in the right direction takes leaders with intelligence, humility, perseverance— any number of traits. Without communication, though, much of this goes unnoticed. Communication shapes employee perceptions of a leader's abilities, commitment, and character.

Communication is a key to collective action. A survey by the American Management Association listed "getting people to work together who have different agendas or goals" as the number-one challenge leaders believed they faced.[4] In most organizations, that's a communication issue. More often than not, people are working at cross-purposes because they lack clarity around direction. Communication gets everybody on the same page, working together to achieve common goals.

Communication enables people to contribute. A plant manager once told us, "If you want to figure out how to run a punch press better, ask the guy who runs it eight hours a day." Employees across every organization possess knowledge the company must have to execute its strategies and achieve results. It doesn't do the company any good if that knowledge is never shared and applied. Leadership communication creates the foundation for employee contributions by providing the perspective employees require to recognize that the information they have is valuable. It also provides a way for employees to share their knowledge with the organization.

Communication is a key to motivation and action. Question: "How many people work at your company?" Answer: "About half." It's an old joke, but all too true in many companies, despite the attention paid to rewards, recognition, job security, working conditions, and the like. Granted, these are important, but intrinsic motivations such as a connection to the substance of work, pride in accomplishment, and belonging to an organization greater than oneself play a critical role as well. Effective leadership communication connects these motivations to strategy and drives action.

In short, leadership communication tells people what they are supposed to do and motivates them to act. It is a key ingredient in every action leaders might take to mobilize employees and make them more effective in strategy execution.

Leaders reorganize their employees into matrix structures and back again. They downsize their organizations and add resources and processes. They change compensation and performance measurement approaches. They immerse their managers in interpersonal skills training. They launch culture-change initiatives. All of these tactics have merit, but communication is critical to all. Communication enables leaders to tap the benefits of reorganization and even of mergers and acquisitions. It leverages compensation and performance management tools. It drives the engaged culture needed to achieve results. In short, although all of these activities can add value, for each of them communication either is fundamental or mitigates the problems the activity addresses. So it makes sense for leaders to address performance issues by improving leadership communication as a first and last resort.

On Strategy communication tells employees what they need to do and why they should take action.

We found this to be true as we worked on one of the more dramatic turnarounds in corporate history. For more than a decade this company, a heavy manufacturer, was a perennial headliner on the *Wall Street Journal*'s list of worst-performing companies. The stock price hovered around $10 per share—down from more than $100 a decade earlier. Market share continually declined along with product quality and customer satisfaction.

Employees said they were victims of events out of their control. Senior leaders and line workers alike believed they were in a "spiral of doom," in which every year they would outline new, aggressive goals and plans but never achieve them. People focused on survival, not success—on assigning blame, not finding solutions. They cut costs to the bone and then cut further, until cost reduction was the only strategy anybody talked about. Then they hired consultants to plot new strategy. They hired new managers to breathe new life and thinking into the organization. They changed bonus structures and organizational designs. All of these efforts floundered until they improved communication.

The CEO began to use leadership communication as a strategic tool to get employees marching in the same direction, excited about where they were going, and *taking action.* In addition to making communication a more important part of their jobs, the members of the company's senior executive team were also given communication responsibilities. The CEO formed a team of informal leaders drawn from up and down management ranks and integrated them into the company's communication approach. He brought together the company's top five hundred leaders every six months to review strategy, progress, and issues, and he required them to communicate to their employees in turn. He reduced complex business planning documents to a short list of critical strategies that people could understand and remember. And he connected execution of those strategies to an outcome that employees throughout the organization all wanted: to again feel proud of their company and the products they built.

When the CEO went to visit employee groups—whether managers or frontline employees—he engaged them in conversations. He would ask two simple questions: "What are we doing that makes you feel proud, and what could we do better?" The conversations connected employee emotions to strategies, but also informed the CEO of business issues. Indeed, those conversations changed the dialogue he had with his own leadership team as well as the communication delivered by the company's publications and other internal communications channels.

Finally, he employed process (as he was an engineer by training, process was his nature). All the executive visits to the operations, the company's publications, the leadership meetings, the messages, and other communication activities were part of a process managed by staff responsible for not only facilitating communication, but also delivering business results.

Strategy became the topic of conversation for employees across the company. They were engaged in their work and achieving results. They knew what to do and did it, and the results followed. Within two years, manufacturing plants increased productivity, efficiency, and quality, and customers saw the difference. The company launched its first major new product line in twenty-five years, and market share jumped. Employees became proud again and focused not on being victims but on driving results. The stock passed $50 per share, *Business Week* named the company one of its "Top Fifty," and the company made the list of the *Wall Street Journal's* top ten best performers.

In the final analysis, the CEO pointed to communication—to getting employees to understand and act on strategy—as the key to success. "You can have plans and strategies and goals and visions and all that stuff," he said. "But until people believe they're winners and believe they can make a difference every day, all that other stuff is not going to get done." He went beyond the babble, led his company with communication that was on strategy, and got results.

SUMMARY

Far too often leadership communication is, in reality, babble. Whether it is long lists of priorities and initiatives or the motivational slogan of the month, in many organizations leadership communication does more harm than good, adding to the confusion and clutter rather than inspiring clarity, focus, and action. It doesn't have to be that way.

The On Strategy philosophy of leadership communication gets rid of the babble and focuses on providing employees with the direction and motivation they need to take action in support of strategy. The On Strategy approach brings simplicity, clarity, and meaning to strategic direction and leverages everyday conversations among managers and employees, when the real work is getting done, to communicate, discuss, and reinforce what needs to be accomplished, how, and why.

Time and time again On Strategy communication has delivered bottom-line results. We've seen firsthand as leaders used On Strategy communication to secure favorable labor contracts, implement an integrated supply chain process, reduce costs, and improve quality. Although communication on its own couldn't have achieved those results, the leaders themselves will attest it was critical to progress—nearly as critical as the strategies and plans themselves. In short, On Strategy communication tells people what they are supposed to do and motivates them to act. It is a key ingredient in every action leaders may take to mobilize employees and make them more effective in strategy execution.

CHAPTER TWO

On Strategy Communication: An Overview

Imagine this scene. A group of people are in a conference room talking with each other about sports, politics, or the latest gossip. The discussion is animated. People share information and perspectives. They laugh and sometimes get a bit tense. But the conversation continues, no matter what—until the meeting starts.

A manager dims the lights and starts a PowerPoint presentation. Conversation stops. Some people pay attention, but eyes begin to glaze over. One person stares out the window; another looks at his shoes. People flip through paperwork brought for the occasion. Another emails on her BlackBerry. The presenter begins to resemble Charlie Brown's teacher in the Peanuts cartoon—"Whah, whah, whah, whah."

Somebody asks a challenging question. The tension in the room rises for a moment. The manager deflects the question. People glance at each other with knowing looks, and the presentation continues. They repeat this routine a few times until the presentation ends. The manager turns up the lights and asks if there are any more questions. People shrug their shoulders, nod, and say, "No—it was all very clear." They stand up and start filing out of the room. The animated conversations start again—about everything but the presentation.

It's a scene repeated in meetings in companies small and large, among senior leaders and frontline employees, in offices and manufacturing plants—most everywhere. You have probably experienced it yourself. The lack of communication and its impact on results is problem enough. The most troubling aspect of the scene, however, is that leaders and employees consider it an acceptable way to operate.

If employees discussed strategy as intensely as politics or last night's baseball game, would results change? You bet they would.

It's not. It's babble, and it's a waste of time and resources. We refer to it as babble because little communication really happened. The leader spoke, but few if any employees were really listening (and if they aren't listening to you, you are babbling). As a result, there was little conversation about the material, no exchange of ideas, and no motivation to take action. There are a number of possible reasons for the employee apathy: perhaps the presentation was confusing and full of jargon, or employees perceived it as irrelevant or at odds with the realities they face, or the presenter's style stifled discussion (as suggested by the increase in tension caused by questions)—the list goes on. Regardless of the reason, the leader's effort to communicate, and the time employees took to attend the meeting, was wasted. If managers and employees were as inefficient at planning, budgeting, or process management as they were at communication, leadership would do something about it.

The On Strategy philosophy, process, and tools provide leaders with a way to improve communication (and avoid lame meetings like the one we just described). It not only delivers leadership's message to the organization so it is inescapable, but it also makes strategy the topic of conversation from the meeting room to the water cooler to the assembly line. The On Strategy approach organizes and articulates leadership's direction so employees can hear it and understand what they are supposed to do. It makes strategy accessible and tangible for employees and connects it to employees' motivations so

When leaders communicate effectively, strategy becomes the topic of conversation across the company.

they take action. Finally, it orchestrates communication as a business process and management discipline.

Leaders implement On Strategy communication in three steps. Step One ensures that leadership's message is about strategy, understandable, relevant, and motivational. We drive On Strategy content with what we call the *Action Equation*: *Know + Feel = Do*. We're no mathematical savants, so this equation is simple: what people know, plus what they feel, inspires them to take the right actions to execute strategy. With this in mind, On Strategy communication first determines what employees have to know and feel in order to act. Then Steps Two and Three prepare for and orchestrate how leaders actually communicate. Through a discipline we call the *People Channel*, leaders from the CEO to frontline supervisors engage employees in conversations to deliver direction, perspective and information, and to pull feedback up from the ranks. In this way, On Strategy communication helps leaders lead.

THE ACTION EQUATION

The Action Equation organizes *what* leaders need to communicate to employees. It begins by focusing a leader's thinking on what employees need to *do* to execute strategy or support the company's position on an issue. Then it expands that thinking to address what employees need to *know* and *feel* so they take the right actions. Moreover, it helps identify what is critical to communicate, and it filters out communication that wastes time or, worse, could be counterproductive to driving action and results.

The Action Equation is homework (and believe it or not, we find it almost as challenging to get leaders to do their homework as it is to get seventh graders to do theirs). It's research and analysis done *before* communication begins. The Action Equation can take some time, but if you skip the work required to adequately inform all three parts of the equation, your communication will be less effective, and you will miss a valuable opportunity to drive execution and results.

Communication on Strategy Begins with *Do*

Informing the Action Equation starts with a leader determining exactly what he or she wants the organization to accomplish and, just as important, what employees need to do to make it happen. These insights are usually found in a company's business plan, but business plans are notoriously poor communication devices. They usually outline all the long-term and intermediate goals, every task, all the numbers everybody has to follow—this is overwhelming to most employees. On Strategy communication focuses leaders on communicating the big goals, the significant activities that will achieve those goals, and how it all works together.

At the outset, On Strategy communication seeks a simple, clear answer to the two key questions every employee is really asking: What are we trying to accomplish, and what do you want me to do? If a leader can't answer those questions in two or three pages of written direction and in a short conversation, he or she isn't ready to communicate (and probably isn't ready to lead).

A CEO of a consumer products company, for example, asked us to communicate his plan to improve company performance to the eight thousand employees his organization comprises. When we asked him to outline the plan, he said he didn't have time to explain it to us, and referred us to a binder that was two inches thick. At that point, the CEO didn't need to communicate. He needed clarity in his own mind about just what he needed his organization and employees to do. If the best direction a leader can give is to send an employee to the library, strategy doesn't have a chance.

The purpose of On Strategy communication is to get employees to Do something. Isn't that what leadership is about?

Lists of goals and metrics don't define what employees are supposed to do either. We worked with an underperforming manufacturing operation that made bath and kitchen fixtures (they called them "after-dinner china"). The plant manager established a list of forty specific metrics for the operation and posted them in every department on white boards that were updated twice a shift. Although his intentions were good, the only outcome of that communication effort was a less-productive work group. The data overwhelmed employees, and the metrics slid downward, along with the morale.

The "vision" (and its sidekick—the "values") isn't necessarily the place to start leadership communication either. Most corporate visions are abstract, well removed from what employees encounter every day, and leave a lot to the imagination. They may be inspirational (we'll get to that later), and they may be good copy for speeches and brochures, but usually they don't tell employees what leaders want them to do.

Leaders must reduce direction to a handful of key objectives and strategies that tell people—the organization—what they are supposed to accomplish and how they should move forward to make it happen. This does not conflict with the school of thought that suggests leaders should provide goals and allow subordinates to determine how to best achieve them (unless that school of thought says "give them a number and let them run").

> *A leader must distill direction to a handful of top priorities. If that's not possible, he or she isn't ready to lead.*

On Strategy communication supports the idea that people closest to a job are well suited to making local decisions. At the same time, leaders must provide boundary conditions that keep the organization on track. Leaders also must provide perspective on the choices employees face in decision making so they know which way to turn when seemingly unsolvable conflicts arise. Finally, good leadership direction—what leaders ask employees to do—should match the leaders' own actions. As they say, if you talk the talk, you have to walk the walk.

On Strategy communication also supports greater engagement and knowledge sharing among employees and leaders, if that's what leaders want employees to do (and we suggest to leaders that's a good idea). For example, one manufacturing executive we worked with gave his direct reports the following direction (what he wanted them to do to reach their goals): work together more collaboratively, put issues on the table for everyone to see and help solve, challenge each other (including the executive), and share knowledge and resources across functions and operations. The On Strategy philosophy says that if you want to create a knowledge-based organization and increase collaboration, you must begin by explaining to people that's what you want in simple, motivational terms.

The *Do* portion of the equation extends beyond strategy to include issues. In today's world, more than ever before, leaders ask their employees to support the company in its relationships with the general public, regulators, political activists, and others. Pharmaceutical companies, for example, ask their employees to publicly support the company when the media scrutinize drug prices, availability, testing, and advertising. Oil companies ask their employees to support company efforts to open new drilling sites and protect against demands for price controls and windfall tax measures. Closer to the business, leaders ask employees for support on issues involving their unions, in reorganizations and during downsizings. In all these instances, leadership is asking employees to *Do* something, whether that's simply staying focused on work or becoming ambassadors for the company among the external publics.

Know Creates Understanding

Leaders inform the *Know* portion of the Action Equation as they determine what they want employees to *Do*. When they frame this direction in the context of the overall organization, they also "connect the dots" for employees between what individuals are doing, what the larger organization is doing, and what's happening outside the organization. These connections enable employees to evaluate activities against overall goals and ensure that they focus on the right activities. It also helps them coordinate with other departments, thereby reducing duplication and conflicting work.

Employees need to know more than what to do and how, though. They need to know the *whys* behind direction—why the selected course of action is the best alternative, and why it benefits them. The first why—understanding the rationale behind strategy—boosts confidence and makes decisions appear less arbitrary. It also reduces the static around strategy execution by changing the conversation employees have about strategy from trying to figure out whether it makes sense, to how they can best execute. That's far more productive. The value of addressing the second why—how strategy benefits employees—is a no-brainer. When employees see a connection between strategy and their self-interests, they pursue it with more intensity, energy, and dedication.

> *Employees need to know what to do and why it's important. That's what On Strategy communication does.*

Finally, some employees need to know more than others do, although those employees are not always at the top of the organizational chart. For example, although everybody should understand a company's brand strategy, employees who touch the customer need to know it in the most concrete terms. These people might be senior managers, but they also might be people on the front line, such as a cashier who talks to customers every day (or snarls at them), or an assembly worker who builds in product quality (or doesn't). If you are executing a new sales strategy, the sales force needs to know more detail about it. If it involves sales mix, production and distribution employees may need to know more, as they will have to adjust to meet changing demands for product. On Strategy communication delivers the depth of information employees need to do their jobs, which differs depending on the strategy and employees involved.

Feel Drives Action

"I'd do this even if they didn't pay me."

A mechanical engineer told us this as he was working on a CAD drawing that looked to us a lot like a pile of spaghetti mixed with little black boxes. An inveterate gearhead, he lived the advice of many self-help books—find what you love to do, then make a living doing it. Leaders must tap into those kinds of intrinsic emotions—what draws people to their jobs besides external rewards—to drive action. And although it may be hard to imagine in many cases, there is something to love in just about every job.

Employees in nearly every situation can have a connection to their work that gives it special meaning. It's about more than pay, recognition, or opportunity (although those things are important). It involves what people do because they want to do it, not just because they are paid to do it. These intrinsic motivations include an affinity for customers and products, energy around the substance of the work itself, and the relationships employees have with their teams. Employees at one health care company, for example, are motivated by helping people and saving lives. Product is the motivating factor at another company, which builds trains—there we saw people actually take less-than-desirable jobs at the old Pullman railcar company so they could have access to mechanical drawings of the original Pullman sleeping cars. The substance of the work motivates employees at a technology company—they are self-described geeks who love solving problems with technology. At many organizations the motivational connections aren't obvious (not everybody can save lives or work on things they are passionate about). Take workers at a fast-food restaurant chain. The motivational connection between an employee, a burger joint, and a $7.50-per-hour job may not be obvious at first. A deeper look reveals more. We worked with one fast-food chain that learned that many employees develop friendships with workmates and feel the positive and negative aspects of peer association. They liked their jobs because they liked the people they worked with. To engage them, the best managers appealed to employees' sense of team. In this situation, the employees didn't give a hoot about whether the burgers were made right or whether customers enjoyed the "brand experience," but they would deliver higher quality or faster service to beat the performance of another crew shift, or so their team could win tickets to a weekend movie opening.

These motivational connections can become much more powerful than incentives such as pay—even in low-paying line jobs. In the course of identifying the team connection that motivated the fast-food workers, we talked to employees at other, local independent fast-food providers, such as mom-and-pop pizza places. Employees at these businesses turned down as much as 15 percent more in pay and better working conditions to avoid joining a McDonald's, Burger King, or KFC outlet—largely because of the team dynamic. One nineteen-year-old worker summarized it for the group. "I work where I do because of the people I work with," he said. "Look, my job sucks. I work at a pizza place, and it gets so hot by the ovens we have a big bowl of ice water we stick our heads into to cool off. But the owner of the business is right there. He goes and gets ice to fill up the bowl. I could get a job at McDonald's or Burger King for a buck more an hour. But I know people who work there. Nobody works together. They all say you're just a body they order around."

Let's not be naive. If these fast-food workers could find better work, they would. We doubt if many would refuse a position that offered more stimulating, cleaner, less stressful work. And quite a few of the employees we interviewed were college kids heading to management careers. But intrinsic factors kept them from jumping to other fast-food jobs for more money. Moreover, the team motivation drove them to work harder and meet goals they otherwise wouldn't think about twice.

On Strategy communication connects strategy to intrinsic employee motivations. Leaders identify what makes their employees tick, then tie strategy to it. That connection results in a more motivated, dedicated work force. The lack of that connection—or worse, a disconnect—is debilitating to an organization. If strategy is at odds with the motivational connections people have with their work and company, they will not support it and they may undermine it. They may oppose it overtly by challenging management, disobeying direction, or pursuing work-arounds that end-run strategy. They may also derail strategy in more subtle ways—by executing a pocket veto of sorts that puts strategic actions low on their list of priorities, allowing simple challenges to become more difficult, and undercutting individual leaders who try to drive strategy.

Finally, just as there are motivational reasons people take action, there are reasons they won't. These "why nots" often involve trust, confidence, commitment, or the organization's culture. They can be rooted in any number of sources, even in the long-past history of an organization. With this in mind, leaders must become "organizational archeologists" of

Just as there are reasons people do things, there are reasons they don't. Identify the root causes of inaction and resistance.

sorts, digging deep into employee experiences to determine why people do what they do—or don't.

We worked with a new vice president of production for a beverage company who was trying to change work practices at one of his operations but was meeting stiff resistance among hourly employees. Working with local managers, we identified the root cause of the problem. Employees charged that ten years earlier, when the operation was acquired from another company, management had lied to them. "They promised us that when we became part of the new company, our health benefits would stay the same," employees said. "In six months, everything changed. We don't trust them."

When we related this to the new VP, his response was: "That was ten years ago. I didn't have anything to do with that. I wasn't even with the company." In reality, their issue was with "management," not him personally. But as a member of management he had to address this trust issue. He visited the operation, gathered employees together in a group, and addressed it head on. "I understand that you believe you were lied to and treated unfairly when the company first acquired this operation. After ten years, I will never be able to get to the bottom of this. Also, I won't be able to turn the clock back and fix those problems. We operate in today's environment, and it's a new ball game. What I will do is believe you and apologize for what the company might have done wrong. And going forward, you can count on one thing: I will say what I'm going to do, and then I'll do what I say, every time." He did, and within a few months employees were ready to support strategy.

"Why nots" can come from any direction, from current issues to times past. Issues may be real or perceived, but their impact is tangible. Leaders must address them in their communication and actions.

The Action Equation (Know + Feel = Do) will take a leader a long way in preparing communication to lead an organization. Well-constructed and articulated communication is meaningless, however, if it doesn't see the light of day. To that end, we've created a process to take the information developed for the Action Equation and deliver it to the organization in an ongoing conversation—in the context of every-day activities, by everyday leaders, every day.

THE PEOPLE CHANNEL

Face it. People take direction from their boss. And people look to their bosses to get answers, perspective, and clarity. If the direction an employee hears from his or her supervisor is different from the direction heard from a manager three levels up—even if it's the CEO—the local boss usually wins. Likewise, if support for strategy is lukewarm among managers and supervisors, it is extremely difficult to generate support at the front line where the rubber meets the road on performance around quality, customer satisfaction, brand delivery, process improvement, and most key metrics. This is nothing new. Research consistently confirms that employees prefer to get information first from their supervisor, and employees tell us this again and again. Therefore, people are the most important communication channel available.

On Strategy communication aligns leaders up and down an organization—the People Channel—to deliver a consistent, strategic message to employees (see Figure 2.1). More than that, it equips them to deliver information in conversation, in the context of local work issues, and "in the moment" when employees ask questions and are making decisions about their work (as opposed to venues

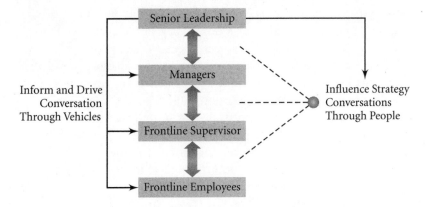

Figure 2.1.   The People Channel Dynamic.

where leaders talk while employees simply wait to get back to doing whatever they were doing before the meeting).

In their role as the primary communication channel, leaders receive training about strategy and how to communicate it. They also are privy to strategic information before the overall organization gets it, so they can deepen their understanding of material and prepare to communicate. Traditional communication channels—the newsletters, conferences, intranet, video systems, satellite broadcast, and other means traditionally associated with leadership communication—play a role, but not center stage. These vehicles exist to support leaders—executives, managers, and supervisors—in how *they* communicate to employees. They distribute a base line of information to the larger organization, helping leaders with the heavy lifting of information dissemination. More than that, however, the traditional channels spark conversations among employees and their bosses; in short, they act as "conversation starters" that help engage leaders and employees in discussions about strategy.

The People Channel isn't about "cascading" information down the management ladder in a rote manner. In this often-referenced approach, managers deliver direction through relatively passive communication. The communication department,

> *People—executives, managers, and supervisors in a company—are the most potent communication channel. Period.*

for example, develops well-packaged presentations and meeting support tools—a "meeting in a box." They provide the materials to managers and supervisors, or make them available on the intranet, and top leaders direct them to communicate. Many times, the canned meetings include videos of senior leaders delivering the message, and local leaders simply play a supporting role.

The weakness of this approach was amplified for us when we heard of the recent experience of one communication executive, as her organization tried to cascade information in the typical manner. As the executive observed, a local manager dutifully played a video, prepared by the communication department, that described the five corporate strategies. Then she asked for questions (there were none). Then the manager pulled up a separate presentation, unrelated to the video, and remarked, "Now, we can talk about what I want to talk about." Although managers' unenthusiastic responses to these "canned" approaches are not always that blatant, it's clear that they don't adequately engage local managers and rarely generate good discussion among employees and leaders, which is critical to effective communication.

The People Channel generates an active interchange of knowledge and ideas among employees and leaders, rather than a passive cascade of information. It provides processes and tools to help engage leaders and employees in an ongoing conversation about strategy, so people have an opportunity to increase their understanding of strategy and offer their ideas and perspectives on how to improve it and execute better. Although the People Channel begins with top leadership, it is ultimately a method to engage managers and supervisors deep in the organization in communication and strategy execution. The People Channel is a process that demands the same kind of discipline required of other strategic endeavors such as planning, budgeting, and process implementation. It is built on the homework conducted through informing the Action Equation and is executed through the following five steps.

Package the Action Equation into a Conversation

When it comes to messages, packaging is critical. Although all of the information and perspective that informs the Action Equation is important, and will be communicated to the organization, it must be organized to promote conversation. That's the purpose of a tool called the Conversation Platform. The Conversation Platform packages the most salient parts of the Action Equation so they are accessible and usable by leaders—all the way to the front line—to drive conversation on strategy. Some call this an "elevator speech." We call it simple clarity.

The Conversation Platform explains strategy in a very short, five-point story. The story starts with where the organization is going, which we call "the cause," because it identifies an outcome that employees want to achieve. Then it articulates no more than four themes that outline how the organization will get there—what employees need to do to achieve the cause. Infused throughout is why all of it is important—to employees and the company. The story is told in words people actually use—not slogans, tag lines, or hyperbole that make communication trite and irrelevant, or the corporate-speak that makes it confusing.

Although the Conversation Platform itself is a very short story, it connects to all of the objectives and activities an organization undertakes to achieve its goals. It provides a context to interpret, evaluate, and understand all of those actions so employees can make sense of and "connect the dots" between where the organization is headed and the activities they see and hear about.

The Conversation Platform is not a list of strategies or a series of PowerPoint bullet points. As a story, it has to hang together. That's because people—leaders and employees—can remember a story, but have trouble remembering lists. A chef can remember a well-planned seven-course dinner, because the menu tells a story: "We'll start with smoked salmon scones and move to a classic Capri salad; then to tournedos portabella,"

People communicate through conversation. On Strategy communication orchestrates those conversations so they drive results.

and so on. The same chef will have trouble remembering more than five or six unrelated items on a grocery list without referring to notes (or the story of his menu). Because we want leaders and employees to have conversations "in the moment," it's important for them to be able to remember what we want them to have a conversation about: strategy. Moreover, people readily have conversations about stories, but don't usually get very excited about lists of things (just as a finely planned meal could spark many conversations, but a grocery list isn't all that compelling).

The Conversation Platform is one of the most potent leadership communication tools in the On Strategy portfolio. In addition to making information more accessible and usable, it helps align senior executive teams and other leaders around a single direction, forms the basis for training leaders up and down the organization, and brings discipline to everyday communication efforts.

Align Leaders Up and Down the Organization

Strategy execution depends on leaders pulling (and pushing) in the same direction. Alignment among leaders can be elusive. The challenges include a lack of information, differing perspectives, misperceptions or misunderstandings about priorities, and varied expectations. On Strategy communication, through the People Channel, helps a top leader align his or her leadership team by simplifying direction, thereby making it understandable and undeniable.

Simplicity is critical to achieving alignment. Simplicity begets clarity, and clarity promotes alignment by making differences among people apparent and actionable. When leaders see that they disagree, they can do something about it. People can't hide behind complexity, feigning agreement while continuing to disagree. They also can't cherry-pick from a long list of strategies and priorities, then pursue those they prefer and ignore the rest. Simplicity brings alignment—or the lack thereof—into the open where leaders can address it.

The Action Equation and Conversation Platform, both of which simplify strategy, are tools that leaders can use to drive alignment at two levels. At senior levels, creating and reviewing the Action Equation focuses leaders on the most important elements of strategy and its rationale, and it promotes robust discussion around strategy. It also considers the mindset of the employee population. Discussions centered on the Action Equation make it more likely leaders will put issues on the table and address them. With simple strategy staring them in the face, it's harder for managers to nod assent to ideas they really disagree with, or to pretend alignment to avoid conflict with superiors, only to "pocket veto" strategy during implementation.

The Conversation Platform provides a tool to align the entire leadership group—down to frontline supervisors. Leaders who are less familiar with strategy find its simplicity refreshing and manageable.

It helps them put all the elements of the Action Equation into terms they can talk about. They can agree with the platform and its underlying assumptions or raise issues. The simplicity and direct nature of the Platform enables them to point out real or perceived inconsistencies with the realities they face.

When coupled with facilitated discussion, the tools of the Action Equation and Conversation Platform become even more powerful. By facilitating discussion, leaders can mitigate some of the deeper challenges that get in the way of alignment. These include internal politics and conflicting agendas, cultural barriers to open and honest discussion, management styles that suppress alternative viewpoints, and real, philosophical differences concerning strategy.

Equip Leaders to Have Conversations On Strategy

One of our clients revamped its internal company university (their learning and training approach). They did a fine job, as evidenced by the extensive course catalogue, the quality of the instructors, and the frequency of offerings. There was, however, one glaring omission. There were no courses on the company's current strategy and how to communicate it to employees responsible for execution.

When leadership decides to launch a new operating process, such as lean manufacturing, they deem learning and training to be essential. The same goes for activities around performance management, budgeting, safety—you name it. Leadership communication on strategy, however, gets meager attention. Unfortunately, many organizations have a blind spot for training executives, managers, and supervisors to communicate strategy, even though strategy execution is probably the single most important endeavor an organization undertakes. One reason for this is a tendency to confuse communication *skills* training with training on communicating *strategy*. Training for public speaking, making presentations, writing memos, and other communication skills is not the same as training to enable communication about strategy.

Leaders up and down the organization must be trained on strategy and how to communicate it. They should be briefed on the background information developed from the Action Equation. This enables leaders to understand the basis of strategy and connect it to employee information and motivational needs. Leaders also must be trained to use the Conversation Platform—through a review of the platform and by role-playing—so they can hone their skills in explaining strategy, influencing conversations with employees about strategy, and engaging employees to provide their knowledge and perspective.

Beyond the strategy-specific training just mentioned, the most effective training related to the People Channel is that which builds interpersonal skills. As we've said, effective leadership communication involves a conversation with the organization, which ultimately translates into conversations between leaders and their employees. The more adept leaders are at having conversations, the better equipped they will be to engage in strategy-related communication.

Leaders up and down the organization must be aligned, equipped, supported, and expected to drive communication about strategy.

Finally, the People Channel must keep leaders abreast of strategic information ahead of the employee population to ensure that leaders have the opportunity to ask questions and clarify issues before engaging directly with employees. This shouldn't be an expensive or complex undertaking. As always, simplicity is key. Leaders can be informed through memos, telephone calls, a dedicated intranet page, and other means that don't require long production times or expense. Communication to them must be continuous and topical, however, and they must be able to ask questions.

Drive Communication and Conversations

The People Channel is most effective when it is coordinated with the other communication vehicles and tactics employed by an organization. These include typical internal communication vehicles, such as the company newsletter, intranet, town hall meetings, and the like. They also include the communication channels integral to operations: the operating meetings, team meetings, reporting documents, budgeting templates, and the other communication vehicles used in the course of conducting business. These communication vehicles support the People Channel in two ways: first, they flood the employee environment with information on strategy, and second, they stimulate conversation on strategy.

Every article, video, meeting, and other vehicle produced to communicate to employees is an opportunity to explain where the company is headed, how it is going to get there, and what employees need to do. This includes routine communication such as personnel announcements, benefits communication, training, and other venues. The individuals creating the material can use the Action Equation and Conversation Platform as prompts to help identify opportunities for communication on strategy, and as filters to determine whether information is relevant to employees.

At the same time, internal communication must be designed to generate conversations. In most organizations, communication is much too bland and safe. It becomes part of the corporate wallpaper; it doesn't make waves, raise an eyebrow, or challenge the norm. Instead, workplace communication should be out-of-the-ordinary and compelling—even controversial and provocative—so people talk about it. Once people are talking, leaders can join in and influence the conversation to support strategy. In this regard, leaders should assess the vehicles used in formal internal communication against their ability to generate conversation. Posters, tent cards, LED signs, and other environmental communication can be very effective at generating conversations. Whatever the vehicle, though, it must be designed with conversation as its purpose, not to look pretty or spout vanilla corporate babble.

The communication department in most companies is an excellent resource for leaders to establish, manage, develop, and support the People Channel. Communication departments usually have writers, producers, and other people to help with the tactics. Some have excellent leadership communication coaches who can be an invaluable resource to the People Channel. It's important, however, to ensure that the communication staff is connected to the business—that they work to drive strategy, not just report on it.

Expect a Lot

We worked with a division president who was frustrated when members of his team didn't follow his example in On Strategy communications—they didn't pick up the ball and run with it. We said to him, "You're the president of this organization for a reason. You understand that communication is a key part of your job. Although there are many great people in this organization, you can't expect them all to act just like you by nature. You need to set expectations for communication."

Expectations around communication, though, are a dime a dozen. Performance management tools raise communication expectations. Communication is often among the list of organizational "values" all employees are supposed to exhibit. There usually is a section in the employee survey on communication. People talk about communication all the time, but communication is usually a secondary consideration in project management and one of the first things managers put on the back burner. Moreover, it's often overlooked as a key requirement in leadership selection and development.

Leaders should expect their subordinates to communicate. Period. The People Channel approach helps set and manage expectations by creating a process and observable steps leaders can manage and monitor. Expectations around communication are clear and measurable. Moreover, at its best the People Channel helps line managers do their jobs by informing and motivating employees to act on strategy and therefore to achieve local objectives. It's part of the job, not another job to do. Every leader should be an active member of the People Channel.

Senior leaders also must set expectations for themselves. On Strategy is a collective effort, but it begins with individuals—the most important being you. Where should you focus your time and effort as it relates to leadership communication? First, manage the People Channel. Set expectations as just outlined, and make sure things happen. Second, prioritize your efforts in terms of the company's strategic communication needs. Review the landscape of the organization and determine which projects and initiatives are the most important to performance. Spend the most time on communication with the employees associated with those priorities. Third, conduct communication activities with a specific purpose in mind—one that supports driving strategy execution. Don't waste time on communication that does not support strategy.

We worked with a company's internal communication team that wanted their executive team to spend more time talking with frontline employees—unskilled laborers who were responsible for moving boxes around warehouses and onto trucks. The company's employee survey revealed that these frontline employees did not understand strategy as well as other groups in the company, and they believed the reason for that was a lack of attention by senior leaders. That made sense, because historically senior leaders were the primary carriers of strategic messages in the company.

We asked two questions:

1. How important is it that the frontline employees understand strategy?

2. If it is important for these specific employees to understand strategy, why don't their frontline supervisors explain it to them? Is there some reason these employees need to hear directly from senior leadership?

The answers to these questions forced the communications staff to consider a different approach. Leadership time is always tight and in demand; it must be used wisely.

At the same time, leaders need to be ready to devote the time necessary to effectively communicate to their organization. Sometimes, On Strategy communication depends entirely on the CEO or other top leaders. This is especially the case when trust issues are involved, or when leaders ask employees to make sacrifices. Effective leaders understand this and make communication a priority even when leadership pressures and time constraints are at their most intense.

SUMMARY

The On Strategy approach to leadership communications ensures that strategy gets out of the binder and becomes a topic of conversation and basis for daily decision making at all levels of the organization. No longer is strategy discussed only at top leadership levels. With On Strategy communication, all employees are engaged in a process to understand strategy, how it affects their work, and why they should take action.

Leaders implement On Strategy communication in three steps. Step One ensures leadership's message is about strategy, understandable, relevant, and motivational. On Strategy content is built with what we call the Action Equation: *Know + Feel = Do*. This is a thought process leaders use to clearly define where their organizations are headed, what they need employees to do in order to execute strategy, and why all employees should be motivated to take action.

Once built, the Action Equation becomes the directional guide for all leadership communication content.

Steps Two and Three of On Strategy communication prepare for and orchestrate how leaders actually communicate. Through a discipline we call the People Channel, leaders from the CEO to frontline supervisors engage employees in conversations to deliver direction, perspective, and information, and to pull feedback up from the ranks. This involves packaging direction into a very simple Conversation Platform, aligning all leaders around direction, setting clear expectations of all managers and supervisors about their role in communication, and providing training, tools, and support.

CHAPTER THREE

Do: What Do You Need Employees to Do?

W hat do you need employees to do? It's a simple question, but many leaders find it very hard to answer. We recently met with the executive team at a mid-sized company that was launching a new strategy. For illustrative purposes, we'll refer to the company as the Land of Oz. They presented the business plan they intended to share with employees. The presentation—only thirteen slides—was short by business plan standards, but was a typical review. There were five goals, such as increase sales to $5.5 billion, achieve 98-percent customer satisfaction, and improve productivity by 7 percent. Those goals resulted in six business outcomes, such as becoming the "most valued supplier of our customers and gaining market share and improving Return on Assets (ROA) to 17 percent." The presentation posed and answered the question "How will we get there?" (The answer: sales growth by market, acquisitions, new products, geographic expansion, product mix—twenty-two activities in total.) Then came the Key Performance Indicators—measures such as net sales, on-time delivery, accident frequency, sales per employee—ten in all. These fed into four value drivers: growth, EBIT, working capital improvement, and ROA improvement. The presentation finished with a discussion of the company's newly developed Lean Strategy, which focused on the customer, developing employees, eliminating nonvalue work, and being a "journey of continuous improvement."

It took about forty-five minutes for the executives to deliver the presentation, and when they were finished, we asked: "Now that we've gone through all that, tell us, what do you need people to do?" There was no answer—just quizzical looks. "We just told you," they said. "Tell us again," we responded. "And do it without slides. Make it simple so we can have a conversation about it." Four hours later, after cutting away the complexity and driving to the heart of their strategy, we finally understood what leadership needed employees to do. They wanted employees to increase efficiency and reduce waste, expand the Land of Oz's customer base and share of spending with each customer, and help integrate new acquisitions into the organization—while always attending to customer satisfaction. All of this would achieve their overall business goals of increasing return on assets and growth.

Why didn't they say so in the first place? Because they hadn't moved from the complexity of their business planning process (which is indeed necessary) to the simplicity required to communicate effectively.

Similarly, we worked at a manufacturing plant where the business plan called for the organization to meet a multitude of metrics. The plant was underperforming in almost every measure, and management needed action, fast. When presented with all the metrics, employees became overwhelmed. They were confused and discouraged; they were not equipped to process all that information. Plant management then winnowed the set of metrics down to five. Discussions with supervisors, however, revealed that even five were too many for the workforce to handle. In the end, management communicated two metrics—one around waste and one around safety. If the plant made progress on these two measures, management decided, it would begin to improve performance across the board. And once performance started to improve, and employees built up their confidence and understanding about how they could affect results, leadership could provide additional direction to refine the progress. It worked.

Good leadership direction tells employees what to do without burdening them with too much detail, while providing enough context to enable employees to make decisions when they run into uncertainty and conflicts. Good direction answers three simple questions: At the end of the day, what are the really important things we need to achieve? How are we going to achieve them? And what do you need me to do? Business plans and lists of metrics usually do not provide good direction. Most business plans are too detailed, and most lists of metrics don't provide context. This may seem to conflict with common understandings of communication that dictate that more is better—that leaders should tell employees everything they can. But simply dumping information on people isn't direction; it's information overload.

Moreover, as we discuss direction, we don't mean to imply that the On Strategy process is a top-down, command approach to strategy development, execution, and communication. As leaders develop their plans, it's clearly in their best interest to enable employees to participate in strategy development and decisions about execution. (We will discuss how to improve participation levels among employees in later chapters.) Once strategy is set, however, it's important that leadership actually lead the organization—that's why leaders are called leaders and get paid more than the rank and file. And clarity in direction and communication is one of the most important elements of effective leadership.

THE ELEMENTS OF ON STRATEGY DIRECTION

On Strategy direction isn't about what you say, it's about what employees hear and do. For employees to be able to hear direction and do something about it, that direction must exhibit four characteristics: it must be simple, actionable, make choices, and match words with actions.

Simplicity Drives Clarity

Try the following test: Write out in five hundred words or less—in the form of a narrative, not a list—what you want your organization to achieve, and how. (Most managers get stuck here.) Then, so you don't fool yourself, sit down with some of your employees—those who will tell it to you like it is. Ask them two questions:

1. Does this make sense?
2. What actions would you take based on this direction?

If they hold conflicting views, don't understand the direction, or can't have a productive conversation about the actions they would take, you have work to do.

An unfair test? Your business is too complex to simplify it that much? Hogwash. The Ten Commandments from start to finish take 309 words—and what's more difficult than morality and humanity? John F. Kennedy outlined his direction to NASA to put a man on the moon in about five hundred words. Is your business more challenging than that? Larry Bossidy and Ram Charan put it well in their book *Execution*: "A leader who says 'I've got ten priorities' doesn't know what he's talking about—he doesn't know himself what the most important things are. You've got to have these few, clearly realistic goals and priorities, which will influence the overall performance of the company."[1] A strategy, they continue, "should be easy to understand. Its essence should be describable in one page . . . If you can't describe your strategy in twenty minutes, simply and in plain language, you haven't got a plan."

> *To have an effective conversation about strategy, it must be simple enough to explain on an elevator ride.*

In response to those who protest that strategy is too complex to reduce to a page, Bossidy and Charan say, "That's nonsense. That's not a complex strategy. It's a complex thought about the strategy. The strategy itself isn't complex. Every strategy ultimately boils down to a few simple building blocks."[2]

Simplicity has always been an important goal, but it has become more pressing as matrix organizational designs replace traditional hierarchies. When employees worked for one boss and orders came down the chain of command, there was continuity and consistency—the list of priorities could be somewhat longer because there was a single boss maintaining focus and balancing the efforts of employees against the priorities. But in a matrix organization, where spans of control are broad and people have multiple reporting relationships, direction can get confusing fast. In fact, General Motors CEO Rick Wagoner pointed to organizational complexity as one reason for GM's many missteps. In addition to geographic units, the company is divided along functional lines, with global groups overseeing areas such as marketing, product development, and human resources.

The system is confusing to most employees and especially so for midlevel employees who have two or more bosses. Wagoner admitted it's difficult: "People really have trouble because they want to know who's in charge," he said. "And the answer is going to be, increasingly: It depends."[3]

With that kind of ambiguity, it's understandable how employees might get confused. That confusion leads to decisions and actions that are off strategy or in conflict, which in turn wastes time, energy, and resources. Employees can only focus on a short list of goals and strategies at any given time. If leaders try to put too many items on their employees' plate, some of those items may fall off. It's inevitable. And if you allow various subgroups of your organization to pick which goals get attention and which take a back seat, you are in for trouble. You can tell if you are engaging in complexity creep by repeating the five-hundred-word test. If you can't tell people what the organization has to achieve, how it will achieve it, and what you want the general employee population to do in five hundred words or less, your "*Do*" message needs work.

The What *and* the How

As leaders construct direction, they often focus on the "what" to the exclusion of the "how." The action that leaders require is implied or ambiguous, and therefore less actionable. On Strategy direction not only sets goals, but also explains how employees can achieve the goals in very concrete, physical, actionable terms. In fact, people can watch good direction manifest itself in real, observable action—something that isn't possible by metrics alone. You can't *watch* revenues increase by $3 billion, but you can watch management acquire a new company, build a new plant, launch a new product, or take any number of actions to generate the revenues. You can't watch sales increase by 10 percent, but you can watch sales people make two hundred additional sales calls to achieve that goal.

If you lead a large organization, it may not be you who is responsible for identifying this kind of actionable direction. (After all, that's why you have a VP of sales, right?) But you are accountable for ensuring that the direction ultimately given to the sales team is, in fact, actionable. If, for example, the goal is set to increase sales by 10 percent, you should expect more from your VP of sales than just to regurgitate that goal to the sales team and hope for the best.

You should expect your senior players to work with their teams and define, with clarity and simplicity, *how* they're going to achieve the goal that's been set. The result is a robust and collaborative plan with far greater chances of success.

The plant manager we mentioned earlier changed his direction to include the "how" in a very physical way. He directed his managers: "Look at your work processes and identify why people are injured and how products are broken. Hold group meetings where employees can contribute their ideas on how to fix the problems. Take action on those ideas within the next thirty days." That's physical direction that you can see people doing. Within weeks, every one of the metrics showed an upward trend.

On Strategy direction is more than lists of priorities and numbers. It provides boundaries and insights about how to get things done.

The concept of physical versus abstract direction goes beyond numbers. We worked with an executive who was pursuing a strategy to move manufacturing from one location to another. The project was critical, and he was worried about it because the organization had failed in a similar move several years before. A key reason for the failure was that the various functions involved had not coordinated their actions well and had even worked at cross-purposes. When we asked how employees were going to do better this time, he said, "With flawless execution." This phrase seems to be a staple among operations people, along with "working with renewed focus; working smarter, not just harder" . . . the list goes on. These phrases aren't leadership communication; they are an easy substitute for a lack of clarity and decisive direction. If you use these kinds of phrases in your direction, replace them with concrete, physical direction. In this case, the executive replaced "flawless execution" with "Communicate across functions through a defined process. Then measure employee confidence that critical issues are being surfaced and addressed to ensure you're on track."

This approach to direction contrasts to some extent, but not entirely, with those that recommend leaders provide employees with broad goals and then let them figure out for themselves how to achieve them. We believe fully in the concept that those closest to work are best suited to make decisions about it. However, leaders must provide boundary conditions to enable those decisions, and they need to provide direction to empower people. That involves an ongoing conversation with employees about direction—not just dictating orders, returning to the corner office, and closing the door. The conversation starts not with a blank sheet of paper, but with a strategic framework of where the organization is headed and how leadership plans to get it there. With such a framework, employees can more constructively and effectively contribute to the plans and eventual success of the organization.

At a minimum, if leaders want employees to make decisions entirely on their own, they need to say so. We've seen situations in which leaders weren't specific about this, and the leaders and their employees were each waiting for the other to make a decision. Beyond that, however, decisions are better informed when leaders provide their knowledge and perspective to the mix. Leaders provide a broader context that local or functional employees don't always have. Leaders often have experience that can improve decisions and avoid mistakes. And by providing well-constructed boundary conditions, leaders actually provide greater empowerment to employees and increase their creativity in decision making. Those boundary conditions could be financial, such as working within budget parameters or against return on asset or margin requirements. They also could include certain fundamentals that are nonnegotiable.

Remember the Nonnegotiables

Sometimes leadership just has to state the obvious, especially when it involves the nonnegotiables. These are tenets and activities fundamental to the company's philosophy of doing business. They govern the organization's decision making, operating approach, and culture. They involve ethics, safety, maintenance, legal process, fairness to customers, respect for employees, and other factors that keep a company on track over the long term. They are often found in a company's vision and values statements. Others simply call them common sense and the right thing to do. In any event, leaders must make them integral to leadership communication and direction, or organizations can overlook, neglect, or ignore them.

The direction Ford Motor Company gave employees when they designed and launched the Pinto compact car in the 1970s ignored the obvious. The story has been well known for years (it's hard for MBA students to avoid it), but the fact that a good part of the company's failure in this instance stemmed from incomplete direction is worth revisiting. Ford CEO Lee Iacocca's direction was clear and simple: the Pinto was not to weigh an ounce over two thousand pounds and not to cost a cent over $2,000. Because of time constraints, tooling for production began before the design and testing phase was complete. As the project unfolded, Ford engineers discovered a major design flaw. Rear-end crash tests revealed that the Pinto's fuel system would rupture easily and cause a fire. The safety implications were clear—people would burn to death (an outcome predicted by Ford risk managers). Engineers considered various alternatives, but the weight and cost of safety didn't fit in, and Ford built the Pinto with the gas-tank flaw. The result: hundreds of people died or were burned badly, the company lost hundreds of millions from lawsuits, and its reputation was irreparably damaged.[4]

Reflecting on the Pinto, Iacocca said, "There is absolutely no truth to the charge that we tried to save a few bucks and knowingly made a dangerous car. The auto industry has often been arrogant, but it's not that callous. The guys who built the Pinto had kids in college who were driving that car. Believe me, nobody sits down and thinks: 'I'm deliberately going to make this car unsafe.'"[5] Tragically, they did build an unsafe car, because the direction Iacocca gave them ignored a nonnegotiable—safety.

Some things must not be sacrificed. Let employees know what those nonnegotiables are.

BP appears to have ignored some of its nonnegotiables—commitments to safety and maintenance—as managers sacrificed the long term for short-term gains. The company was investigated in 2006 following an explosion in a Texas refinery that cost a number of employee lives. According to reports, BP leaders pressured operating managers to boost margins, but did not explore safety implications with vigor. "The prevailing culture . . . was to accept cost reductions without challenge and not to raise concerns when operational integrity was compromised."[6] During the same period, BP failed to maintain its oil pipeline in Prudhoe Bay, and 250,000 gallons of crude oil spilled onto the Alaskan landscape. According to reports, the company had reduced inspection personnel and ignored warnings by contractors about corrosion. Local managers went so far as to intimidate employees who raised concerns about the pipeline.[7] Nonnegotiables around safety and maintenance are certainly visible in BP general communication such as the company's vision and values, but apparently leadership at the company did not stress them in their specific direction, or through their actions, to the extent necessary.

NASA experienced a similar deterioration of its nonnegotiable around safety, which resulted in the crash of the Space Shuttle *Columbia*. According to the Columbia Accident Investigation Board (CAIB) Report, "Streamlining and downsizing, which scarcely go unnoticed by employees, convey a message that efficiency is an important goal. . . . When paired with the faster, better, cheaper NASA motto of the 1990s and cuts that dramatically decreased safety personnel, efficiency becomes a strong signal and safety a weak one. This kind of doublespeak by top administrators affects people's decisions and actions without them even realizing it."[8] Contrast that to the direction President Kennedy gave to NASA at the outset of the Apollo program: "I believe this nation should commit itself to achieving the goal, before this decade is out, of landing a man on the moon and *returning him safely to earth*" [our emphasis]. A safe return from a mission may seem too obvious to mention in a presidential address, but as it turns out, Kennedy was prescient in his direction. In short, unlike Kennedy in his first direction, NASA leadership did not provide direction to the organization that put safety as high a priority as other objectives. Over time, a drift in direction made it a secondary consideration, not by design but by default. In the end, the Space Shuttle Columbia crashed despite warnings about safety and last-minute protests by engineers on the scene.

As you provide direction to your organization, it's important to consider how execution against that direction will affect the nonnegotiables. This doesn't mean leaders must list all the company values, operating mandates, and other nonnegotiables in every communication. Besides being tedious, that approach wouldn't work anyway. When repeated in rote fashion, even the most compelling of the nonnegotiables becomes babble. Leaders, however, must ensure that they adequately represent the nonnegotiables in the body of communication they deliver. They also must emphasize the nonnegotiables at times when they are relevant to the work at hand. For example, designing an automobile would probably not put nonnegotiables such as maintenance at the factory or the meeting of accounting standards at risk. However, automobile design and safety are inseparable, so it's not only relevant but also necessary to address that nonnegotiable in leadership direction and communication about that design. Ford's Iacocca should have said: "The Pinto must not weigh an ounce over two thousand pounds, must not cost a cent over $2,000, and must achieve a safety standard you would want for your own daughter." This would have saved a lot of lives and problems for his company. The same would undoubtedly hold true for BP and NASA if leadership had put greater stress on the nonnegotiables in their business.

Make the Courageous Choices

Much of the direction leadership provides to employees is cowardly. This may seem a harsh judgment, but we've found it to be true. Essentially, leaders tell employees to simultaneously achieve two goals that come into conflict—say, volume production and quality, or increased revenues and increased margins, or higher prices and higher market share. Giving this kind of direction is like asking employees to turn left and right at the same time: it just isn't possible. But leaders ask it anyway. "Both are important," they say, and cede the decision to employees.

As a result, the company gets what line employees determine is more important (usually by trying to figure out what management wants), and this causes problems. For example, when managers say quality and volume are both important, and don't say which is ultimately *more* important, employees aren't sure what to do when they see a quality issue. They must decide whether they should address it despite the fact that it would reduce production volume. Because management has avoided this conflict by deciding to both ensure quality and increase production volume, employees, not management, make the choice between the two priorities.

Leaders should make the critical choices, not every individual employee.

They usually do this not by thoughtful deliberation but by interpretation of what they think management wants. In essence, they try to read their leaders' minds. Unless you have a large team of astrologists, tarot card readers, and psychic supervisors, that's no way to run a business.

We witnessed this in an engineering function for which leaders stressed both process and speed in product development. They told engineers that the new development processes, which were designed to eliminate a history of design flaws, were inviolate. At the same time, the leaders were pressuring the engineers to produce designs faster: "We need a greater sense of urgency, and we must hit our schedules." In time, the engineers inevitably faced a choice: maintain process discipline and deliver designs late, or shortcut the process to meet schedules. That's not a decision that three hundred engineers should be making independently.

It's likely that employees at BP, Ford, and NASA faced difficult choices when they considered short-term objectives and longer-term needs of the business. *Do I make my cost-reduction target and reduce the pipeline maintenance budget, or do I miss the financial target and continue high standards of maintenance?* Certainly, top leadership wants both. But at some point that wasn't going to happen, so which action takes priority? Most of the time, employees make that determination by selecting either the path of least resistance (and least criticism by management), or the path they've taken before, or the path that will delay the day of reckoning. Good leadership makes the tough strategic choices instead of leaving them to such chance.

Match Words and Actions

Effective leadership direction is consistent with the realities employees face every day. All too often, we hear about situations in which leadership's words and actions are at odds. Managers say, "Customer service is our most important priority," for example, but then they lay off customer service employees. They say, "Cost reduction is nonnegotiable," but then they give themselves hefty raises and bonuses. When words and actions don't match, employees follow the actions. An effective leader makes sure actions and words match.

One way to do this is to deconstruct your strategic planning documents and budgets across functional silos. This is a process in which you list all of the budget and resource allocations, as well as all of the initiatives, against each of the goals and strategies you are communicating. For example, you may have cost reduction and quality strategies. List everything your organization is doing across all functions about cost in one column, and likewise everything that's supporting quality in another column. The resulting lists will show whether your strategy is more talk than action.

We did this for one consumer products organization, for example, and found enough activities under cost to fill several pages. By comparison, quality and customer satisfaction strategies specified scant few activities. This exercise prompted management to reevaluate some of its activities. From a leadership communication standpoint, we did less talking about quality and customer satisfaction until actions caught up to the words. This avoided communication that would have hurt employee trust and confidence in leadership. Leadership also revisited its programs and resource allocations concerning quality and customer satisfaction in order to ensure that they were adequate (they weren't).

> *Actions speak louder than words. Their impact on communication can't be ignored.*

Sometimes the disconnect that employees perceive between leadership's words and actions really is only a matter of perception. We worked with one company, for example, whose employees were complaining that management was cutting back on training, and that these cutbacks were affecting their ability to do their jobs right. In reality, training was as robust as it always had been, but the company was delivering it in a less visible way. They had discontinued outmoded training approaches, for example, and replaced them with alternatives such as on-line training. Employees didn't see people filing in and out of training rooms, so they thought there was less training going on. Leaders corrected this misperception through more concerted communication and were able to mitigate employee dissatisfaction about training.

Being more disciplined about matching actions to words leads to a simple but effective communication approach that helps leaders build credibility and trust: words-actions-words. In this approach, leaders tell employees what they or the organization will do, point out the actions as they are under way, and then remind employees that the completed action was the one the leader spoke of in the first place. This "bookend" approach to leadership communication is very effective in making sure employees know how elements of strategy fit together and that words and actions match.

SETTING A CLEAR PATH FOR THE LAND OF OZ

Translating a thick binder that houses strategic direction into a brief document that reflects the elements of good direction is a challenge. To help leaders to meet this challenge, we've developed four key questions that will organize your thinking and focus communication on key direction.

- What are the "critical few" goals we need to achieve?
- What are the nonnegotiables we need to protect?
- How will we as an organization achieve these goals?
- Do our words and actions match?

If leaders answer these four questions in simple, clear terms, they can create direction that employees and the entire organization can follow. The executives at the Land of Oz found the exercise revealing. (The review represents the actual case, but we've disguised it to protect confidentiality, and we've taken a few liberties to clarify it as an example.)

What Are the "Critical Few" Goals We Need to Achieve?

These are the goals that will make or break you; the ones that, when achieved, will influence the rest. Answering this question requires leaders to raise their perspective from ten thousand feet to thirty thousand feet, so they can see how the pieces fit together and can determine the overarching requirements of strategy execution. The executive team at the Land of Oz started with five goals. We asked the four questions listed in Table 3.1 to raise their thinking to the thirty-thousand-foot level and better focus their goal setting. As we said earlier, simplicity is critical to good direction, so fewer goals are better than more. And although all the goals are important, and leadership may want to monitor them to enable midstream course corrections, it isn't necessarily effective to make *all* the goals

Full Set of Goals	Focusing Questions	Critical Few
$5.5 billion in sales	Which goals will be the result of your efforts?	17% ROA
Improve operating margins by 20 to 25%		$5.5 billion in sales
Accumulate $250 million of capital	Which goals aren't up for debate? (If you don't hit them, you will not be successful.)	
17% ROA	Which goals will be achieved as part of the effort to achieve the results? (These are not the critical few.)	
Improve inventory turnover by 15%		
Improve productivity by 5%	Which are the critical goals you need to achieve?	

Table 3.1.   Finding the "Critical Few."

the focus of communication—just the ones that really count. The executive team settled on two: sales and return on assets. Moreover, they decided that if they had to choose between the two, the ROA goal would take priority. They had to grow, but they had to grow profitably. In addition, a significant part of the growth would come from acquisitions, which top leadership would monitor closely, so they wanted to make sure the rest of the organization delivered profitable growth. These were the goals that would make or break the company over the long term.

What Are the Long-Term Nonnegotiables We Need to Protect?

The Land of Oz executives revisited their initial direction to the organization and added reinforcement to the nonnegotiables that were important to the company's health. There are always tradeoffs, and it's a leader's job in the direction he or she provides to enable employees to make the right choices in those tradeoffs. For the Land of Oz, the top nonnegotiable was ensuring that it maintained its strong relationships with customers by continuing to deliver high levels of service.

The executives believed that the focus on growth and returns posed risks to long-standing and productive relationships with the company's current customers, which was one of the company's nonnegotiables from its inception. They also considered the impact of their goals

What are the "critical few" goals we need to achieve?	17% ROA$ $5.5 billion in sales
What are the nonnegotiables we need to consider?	Maintain high levels of customer satisfaction

Table 3.2. Remembering the Nonnegotiables.

on other nonnegotiables, including safety and ethical behavior. The executives believed that ethical operating practices were well established and monitored by current systems and that these issues did not have to be a focus of leadership communication at the time. One of the company's strategies, Lean Manufacturing, was very oriented toward safety, so that nonnegotiable would be integral to leadership communication going forward. However, distractions relating to the acquisition could threaten customer relationships. Also, as employees pushed for higher returns on sales, there was a risk that they could sacrifice customer satisfaction. To mitigate these risks, the leadership group made customer satisfaction one of the cornerstones of their communication approach, as depicted in Table 3.2.

How Will We as an Organization Achieve These Goals?

The answer to this question outlines the strategic actions the organization is pursuing to achieve the goals. By strategic actions, we mean the physical steps the organization must take, not another set of goals. (We've been in meetings where executive teams spent hours debating the difference between a goal and a strategy. Our recommendation— at least from a communication standpoint—is to forget the debate and simply answer the question, how are *we* going to achieve our goal? And do it by identifying actions you can observe people doing.)

Again, the answer has to be simple—the handful of key actions the organization will take to achieve the critical few goals. These should be the large-scale activities that outline strategy. If it isn't a critical driver, leave it off the list. For the Land of Oz, the actions unfolded as outlined in Table 3.3.

Note that each of these "hows" is an observable action. Instead of listing more metrics that people had to achieve, leadership cited actions the organization needed to take to deliver on the goals.

What are the "critical few" goals we need to achieve?	17% ROA
	$5.5 billion in sales
What are nonnegotiables we need to consider?	Maintaining high levels of customer satisfaction
How will the organization achieve these goals?	Implement lean manufacturing systems
	Introduce new training that focuses on cost reduction
	Trim non-value-add staff
	Extend lean manufacturing ideas to nonmanufacturing workers to cut costs
	Expand capacity
	Grow geographically
	Add new customers
	Introduce new product lines to existing customers
	Shift the product mix for builders in key markets
	Add new product lines
	Acquire companies in new areas with customers we don't have
	Monitor a small set of key metrics and connect them to performance management and bonuses

Table 3.3.   Bringing the How to the Do of the Equation.

Do Specific Activities Support the Strategic Actions, or Not?

The executives then drilled one step deeper. They made certain the specific local initiatives, resource allocations, and functional activities the organization pursued actually supported the actions they outlined. This was a revealing part of the exercise, as the executives saw they did not have enough emphasis on their nonnegotiable of customer satisfaction. Indeed, as a result of this exercise, management decided to add another metric to their list of key metrics that would be monitored: a customer satisfaction index. Previously the company had measured customer satisfaction by on-time delivery. This was inadequate to the job, so they decided to include other factors and compile them into an index. The types of activities the executives outlined for three of the twelve strategic actions are listed in Table 3.4 as an example.

Strategic Actions	Specific Activities
Implement lean manufacturing systems	Acquire a suite of new tools (including 5S, TPM, visual management, SMED, batch size reduction, cellular manufacturing, standardized work, work balancing, production leveling/smoothing, and point-of-use systems)
	Train employees on these new tools
	Reward employees for participation in the training
Add new customers	Implement new marketing initiatives
	Add a senior position in the organization to coordinate sales and marketing activities
	Add seventy-five sales people
	Implement new sales management training programs
Monitor a small set of key metrics and connect them to performance management and bonuses	Net sales
	Customer satisfaction index
	Accident frequency
	Sales per employees
	AR percent current
	Days sales outstanding
	Velocity of inventory
	Days payable outstanding
	PBOP per employee

Table 3.4.   **Linking Strategy to Activities.**

With this work, the executives were able to identify, in simple, concrete terms, what the organization needed to accomplish and how it was going to get there—what employees had to *Do*. Now they had to give them reasons why they should.

SUMMARY

Effective direction begins with telling employees what the organization needs to accomplish and how, and what the employee population is supposed to *Do*, which is one part of the Action Equation: Know + Feel = Do. It's very actionable—the difference, for example, between telling the sales force they need to increase revenues by 10 percent (an outcome) and telling them they each need to make two hundred additional sales calls (an action). Good direction also makes the tough decisions between priorities, as opposed to putting them all on an equal footing and making employees decide, when they come into unavoidable conflict, which is more important. For example, good direction tells employees that ultimately quality is more important than volume, customer satisfaction is more important than cost reduction, and growth is more important than margins (or vice versa), so they make the right decisions when they have to. Finally, good direction also includes specifics around critical outcomes of nonnegotiables such as safety, maintenance, customer satisfaction, and ethics. These are the kinds of things that leaders may assume they can take for granted but can be compromised as employees pursue other goals—sales, returns, efficiency, and the like—that are more dominant in communications (and in performance management tools, recognition, advancement, and so on).

Effective direction is simple. To quote the old adage, it's more like telling employees what time it is than telling them how the watch works. Business plans usually outline all the goals, objectives, strategies, initiatives, and resource allocation—the workings of the whole watch. Because of their complexity and length, they are not good communication documents (even though they may be great planning tools). Therefore, leaders must simplify direction into a handful of key concepts they must communicate. In fact, good direction usually can be distilled into a message of five hundred words or less that simply tells employees what the organization needs to accomplish and how, and what the employee population is supposed to do.

Finally, yet important, good leadership direction is about what leadership does, not just what it says. Words and actions have to match. This means the objectives leadership stresses in communication must be backed up by resource allocation, initiatives, attention, and compensation—the concrete actions employees see that make the talk walk.

CHAPTER FOUR

Know: What Do Employees Need to Know to Take Action?

—〜〜— 66 **I**f you just told me that crooked labels were no good, I could have saved us a lot of money."

That's what an employee told her supervisor when technicians started to install an expensive new camera system on her beer bottling line. The camera would spot crooked labels and sort them out of production.

"I stand here all day and watch them go by," she said. "It wouldn't be hard to pull them."

She just hadn't known that crooked labels were a problem—or at least that they were *her* problem. A manager might think it's obvious—a crooked label is a crooked label. The employee had a different perspective, though. "The beer is still good," she said. "Who would throw out perfectly good beer because of a label?"

She has a point. She didn't know that distributors objected to bottles with crooked labels, or that they were outside quality standards ("You can't tell a good beer by its label," she'd say.) Nobody had told her it had to be done—or why it was important.

Ensuring that employees know what they are supposed to do is a fundamental purpose of leadership communication. That process begins, as we described in Chapter Three, with identifying where the organization is headed and how it's going to get there. In the

Strategy has to make sense to employees and intersect with their interests.

example just introduced, quality production would have been on the list of what employees must *Do.* If leaders communicate this alone, they will be ahead of many companies. But there's more to leadership communication than that.

Employees need to know the *reasoning* behind goals and strategies. Without it, they strive to find answers themselves—from each other, in chat rooms, by reading the newspapers, by talking to neighbors—you name it. This haphazard approach wastes a lot of time (much of it on the job) and often results in misunderstandings and misdirection—and even wasted beer.

Moreover, some employees need to know more than others do. Although the whole organization must be devoted to strategy execution, there are groups of employees that have a disproportionate impact on specific strategies. These could be small groups of specialists such as engineers, marketers, or operations people. They might be the level of the organization that sets strategy or the employees deep in the organization who implement it. Leaders need to prioritize their employee audiences based on their relative importance to successful strategy execution.

THEY NEED TO KNOW WHY

The days when people just did what you told them to are long gone (actually, was it ever that way?). Before employees truly commit to action, they ask the "why" questions:

- Why are we headed in this direction?
- Why is it important to the business?
- What's in it for me?
- Why did we pick that strategy instead of another?
- Why must we change? *or* Why don't we change?
- Are we still on course?

The list goes on.

Answering the "why" questions is worth the extra work it takes. A full understanding of the "whys" provides context that helps employees set priorities and communicate knowledge they have that could help others in the organization do their jobs. An understanding of the "whys" helps employees connect their jobs to enterprise-wide activity—creating a "line of sight" between their work and that of the larger organization. And conversations driven by the "why" questions inform leadership as well as employees about substantial issues and nuances of execution. They force deeper evaluation of goals and strategy, and they generate healthy dialogue that challenges assumptions and drives creativity.

Employees often pose questions around financial targets. For example, the Land of Oz set its goals at $5.5 billion and a 17-percent ROA. Employees will ask, "Why did leadership pick those numbers? Why $5.5 billion? Why not $7 billion? Or $3.5 billion?" These are fair questions. The numbers have to make sense to employees, and people need to understand the consequences of success and failure. Conversely, if the numbers appear to be arbitrary or to serve only management, employees will not believe they are important or pursue them with intensity.

The leadership at one manufacturing company, for example, wanted to implement a number of efficiency programs but met stiff resistance among employees. Employees believed management's decisions were arbitrary and even counterproductive to efficiency issues they experienced. For example, employees in the finishing department told management, "If you want to improve efficiency, why don't you buy new equipment? The equipment we are using is older than we are." The answer to that question revolved around the need to achieve ROA hurdles, which new equipment would not deliver. In response, leaders included discussions of ROA in their regular communication. They explained why it was important to achieve that particular financial metric (the cost of capital needed to operate the business), and why it was important to employees (hitting that target keeps the plant viable). They presented the information in terms that employees could relate to their personal experiences, such as managing their checkbooks, going to the bank to get a mortgage, and the like. The company also created a training program that showed employees—from plant management to assembly line workers—how to calculate ROA for investments and activities undertaken at the plant (and, yes, line employees can understand finance). As employees understood the reasons behind the numbers, they embraced leadership's efforts to control costs.

Knowing Goes Both Ways

The person closest to a job usually knows the most about it, whether it's frontline work or managerial tasks like planning, process management, and budgeting. Because of that, leaders can learn a great deal from the people working in their organizations. Conversations revolving around the "why" questions create the dialogue necessary to challenge bad decisions, and to stimulate new, creative thinking at all levels of an organization.

We worked with a manufacturing company whose senior VP of operations decided to cut costs by reducing the workforce by about 20 percent. He believed the company's manufacturing operation was overstaffed; he wanted an immediate reduction in force. The managers below him knew that a force reduction that aggressive would shut operations down—they just couldn't

Employees know their work better than most leaders. Listen to them.

handle it. The senior VP and operations management never had that conversation. The senior VP held a Ph.D. and wasn't one to listen to mere mortals. They made the cuts, and operations fell apart. It took months to repair the damage, the company lost millions, customers were incensed, and the Ph.D. was out of a job.

This is an extreme example, but the lesson is clear. Employees know something about their work, and listening to them can prevent nasty mistakes and create breakthrough levels of performance. Conversations, based on an informed workforce, are the most effective means of making this happen. This may seem to be an obvious statement, but such productive conversations—in which manager and employee actually exchange ideas—are more the exception than the rule. On Strategy communication addresses this issue.

Questions Go Beyond Goals and Strategy

"I don't tell people I work for a chemical company. It's too embarrassing." That's what some employees who work for some major chemical companies say about their jobs. They fear the skeptical looks of neighbors and the endless questions about whether a Love Canal or Bhopal-type disaster is possible in their community. Difficult questions also plague big oil and pharmaceuticals. It gets particularly challenging when Hollywood gets involved. After the release of the film *The Constant Gardener,* a fictional account of drug testing in third-world companies, the questions fielded by employees at pharma companies were all too real. Nobody likes to answer a question like, "Does your company use poor people in African villages as guinea pigs?" And as oil prices continue to rise, oil company employees feel like they are the people over a barrel.

Issues of public concern can affect any industry. People first snubbed U.S. auto companies for their long slide in competitiveness, and now vilify them for poor mileage standards and their contribution to global warming. Employees at utilities are considered fair game. Does anybody give the local telephone or cable company a break? Even the local retailer is in the line of fire as people in communities ask about their hiring of illegal immigrant workers, the absence of health care benefits, and low wages.

Besides these public issues, companies must deal with issues specific to their operations. Employees consider whether to unionize or not. They challenge management about diversity in the workplace. When the CEO makes as much as five hundred times the pay of the average line worker, people question the ethics and fairness of leadership—especially in the wake of scandals like those of Enron and Tyco. They fear for their future security when they see pensions at other companies evaporate because of corporate mistakes or malfeasance. Employees can't be blamed for questioning the judgment or motives of their leadership team when they read about a CEO who allegedly had his company purchase a $30 million apartment with $6,000 shower curtains, or pay a million dollars for his wife's birthday party—complete with an ice sculpture of Michelangelo's David. All of a sudden the company's corporate jet, the spacious executive offices, and the salaries listed in the proxy statement become much more suspicious, and employees want to know much more about them.

> *On Strategy communication deals with issues that affect strategy, not just the strategies themselves.*

Such issues have serious consequences. When the public turns against a company or industry, government watchdogs and regulators usually aren't far behind. (To counteract this, employees can play a role in supporting the company if they are well informed and on the company's side.) Moreover, public scrutiny and attacks can have a demoralizing effect on employees, which has implications for attracting and retaining talent and productivity. Because of this, leaders must be prepared to go beyond business as usual in their communication and to tackle controversial issues as they arise. Bottom line, if leadership wants employees to support the company with the various external publics that might influence the company's ability to pursue strategies, they must answer "why" questions that extend beyond the strategies themselves.

Answering the "Why" Questions

Employees want answers to the "why" questions at two levels. The answers not only must make sense from a business standpoint but also must relate to employee interests. Leadership must be able to explain the business rational for goals and strategies and then relate how achieving progress on them benefits employees.

Business leaders often connect strategy and financial goals to shareholders or to the company's share price. We've yet to see an employee jump out of bed for the sake of the shareholders. Generally, this is not a relevant or powerful connection for employees, even if they own stock. In fact, studies show that employee stock ownership affects company performance not so much because of employees' equity connection to their companies, but because employees in companies with stock ownership plans are better informed about how the company operates.[1] Essentially, companies with large, stock-owning employee populations do a better job communicating to them. The major factors that employees usually want to understand (or that leadership must get them to understand) include the following:

COMPETITIVE FACTORS. Employees readily understand the pressures of competition. They see it in their own lives and can transfer that experience to that of their company. Leadership, however, must make the connection between competition and the strategies they have selected. One company pursued a cost-reduction strategy as a defensive measure. Competitors were undercutting them on price, and leadership needed flexibility to meet the threat. Employees were lackluster in their support when leaders first outlined the strategy as a cost-reduction measure alone. When the leaders reframed it as a competitive move, however, employees embraced the strategy and executed it with intensity. They could relate to the threat to the business posed by lower-cost competitors, but not to cost reduction as an end in itself (cost reduction often seems to translate into fewer jobs for line employees and higher bonuses for top leaders—a bad combination for motivation).

SOCIETAL ISSUES. Technology, globalization, demographics, geopolitics, the price of oil, government actions—even the weather. If these trends affect your business, and in turn drive strategy development, employees need and want to know about them. They provide a powerful rationale for leadership's direction that relates to issues employees care about. We worked with an insurance company, for example, that based its new strategy on the changing demographics of its market. The baby boom generation was aging, and financial planning was of greater importance to them than buying life insurance. Therefore, the company wanted to transform its sales force from one that focused just on selling insurance to one that provided comprehensive financial advice and products. This required significant new training and the will among sales people to change their relationship with their customers. They wouldn't do it unless they had a good reason why, and that reason was based in the business environment—demographics.

INDUSTRY TRENDS. Each industry has its own set of opportunities and challenges, and those can provide powerful reasons for the goals and strategy leaders select for their companies. These go beyond just competition to involve industry-wide trends. Industries undergoing consolidation present a specific challenge to the companies in that industry. The same holds true for industries as they change distribution from bricks-and-mortar to web-based channels or from direct-to-customer to resellers. Some industries go global, some stay local. Whatever the trends, they can provide powerful reasons for strategy decisions. Leaders must share that perspective with employees.

CUSTOMER FACTORS. Demands, preferences, whims—whatever the motivational factors that influence customer decisions to do business with your company, these can be key to strategy. A computer supplier, for example, realized that customers wanted to buy more than a computer; they wanted to buy a solution to a business problem. Thus the company needed to shift its business strategy from delivering equipment to providing solutions to technology problems. To transform itself from an equipment supplier to a solutions provider, the company started acquiring new businesses with that capability and began placing less emphasis on traditional, transactional sales. This resulted in discontent among longer-tenured employees. Leadership had to provide a strong business rationale for the move: they explained that customers were demanding this capability and would go elsewhere if they didn't have it. Employees understood this to be a threat to the company's future; once they knew this, they supported the new strategy.

The list of "whys" can be quite lengthy. As you plan and execute leadership communication, articulate the answers around why the goals and strategies you are pursuing make sense. Employees will want to know.

WHO NEEDS TO KNOW?

Leaders throughout the company—from executives to frontline supervisors—should know strategy. Period. When leaders up and down the organization all have an aligned, solid understanding of goals and strategies, they can translate that knowledge into action throughout the organization. Moreover, they are in a position to listen to employees at a local level and incorporate that knowledge into decision making and execution.

Yet most leaders beyond the top echelons are in the dark. We worked with a company that was trying to grow by more than 30 percent in two years. Management set seven strategies to accomplish the goal, including a shift in sales mix and the pursuit of new customer segments. They conducted typical communication activities to mobilize employees behind the strategies, including town hall meetings; a special brochure that outlined the company's vision, values, and strategies; coverage in the company magazine; posters in every lobby and hallway; and the like. As a person in the Communication Department put it, "If you don't know the strategies by now, you've been asleep."

Well, the snoring was deafening. According to employee surveys, 35 percent of the employees didn't know what the strategies were.

That might not have been a big problem if those employees were the janitorial staff, but that wasn't the case. In fact, the people most directly charged with managing strategy execution day-to-day—the director level of the organization—formed the group *least* informed about strategy. More than 40 percent of that group said they were uninformed about strategy, according to the survey. Making the situation even worse, the most ill-informed group resided in the sales organization, which was charged with executing the most critical elements of the company's growth strategy. If fewer than six out of ten of your key people don't know what the organization is supposed to do, what is the chance it will happen? If four

Every employee should have a baseline understanding of strategy. You never know who will contribute the breakthrough idea or the critical piece of information.

of the players on the field in a football game didn't know the play, would it work? (We live in Chicago, and from watching the Bears in the year they went 1–13, we can attest to the fact that it doesn't.)

The lack of understanding of goals and strategies at management levels of a company surprises many leaders. But it's not hard to uncover it. Employee surveys usually track understanding of strategies. However, it's very important to look at how well specific groups scored in the survey, because some groups are more important than others. Certainly, if leadership levels at the top of the organization are uninformed about strategy, it's less likely employees further down the line will know what they are supposed to do to make strategy reality.

If questions about strategy are not in an employee survey, simply ask managers what they think the strategies are. Gather the top twenty to fifty people in your organization, pass out index cards, and ask them to answer the question, "What are our business goals and how do we expect to achieve them?" Make sure you ask about not just financial goals (people often get that right) but also strategy—how the organization expects to achieve its goals. Make the process anonymous, so it is not threatening and so people write down what they believe, not what's written in some corporate pamphlet. Moreover, this is not a test for employees; it's a test for leadership—to determine how well they have communicated on strategy. Collect the cards and see what they reveal. In most organizations, the wild variations in the answers will be startling.

Some employee groups need to know more than others, even within leadership ranks. Certain groups of employees have a disproportionate impact on strategy execution, and leadership must consider this as they communicate about strategy. Research and development people, for example, have a significant impact on strategies involving innovation and product leadership. Employees in manufacturing have a significant impact on quality and cost strategies. Employees who interface directly with customers are often the primary drivers of customer satisfaction and brand delivery strategies. Leaders must identify these groups and communicate more aggressively with them.

For example, we worked with a heavy vehicle company to deliver a new brand strategy, and we identified engineers responsible for new product development as a group key to strategy execution. We found the engineers understood the "top line" of the brand strategy—products had to be "dependable" and "comfortable."

But the engineers really didn't know what these terms meant—they needed to know more in order to do their jobs. "Is dependable five hundred thousand miles?" they asked, "or a million miles without a major breakdown that takes it out of service? And what constitutes operator comfort? A nice seat? A nice ride? And how nice?" The

> *Some employees are more important to strategy than others. Communicate accordingly.*

entire organization didn't need to know these details, but the engineers did. Without that kind of direction, they couldn't do their jobs.

Answering these questions took a bit of creativity. The marketing people came up with an answer to the dependability issue: "More dependable than any other competitor product at a competitive price." That gave the engineers a boundary condition they could work with, and it put parameters around the relationship between dependability and cost (they said they could build a product that lasted a million miles, but it would cost an awful lot). The "customer comfort" direction was a bit more difficult. "It was kind of like explaining what the color red looks like," said one of the marketing consultants. "You know it when you see it." To see it, engineering leadership took the direction in their own hands—literally. They used the trucks they had designed as their day-to-day personal vehicles, and they learned what operator comfort was all about. Design changes flowed. And when the company launched the new products, customer reaction was very favorable, the product set the standard for innovation in the industry, and the company realized an immediate increase in market share.

Everybody in an organization should know where the company is headed and how it's going to get there. Some employees, however, need to know more in order to do their jobs. Leadership must communicate on strategy to those groups in deeper, more actionable terms.

Do	Know
17% ROA.	Know what to do, plus why.
$5.5 billion in sales.	The company needs to grow to keep costs low and to accumulate the cash we need to keep investing in ourselves. It also will provide an appropriate return to our shareholders. We have an obligation to them, and a high share price helps us when we want to acquire other companies with stock.
Maintain high levels of customer satisfaction.	
Implement lean manufacturing systems.	
Introduce new training that focuses on cost reduction.	
Trim non-value-add staff.	We are in a commodity-type business—if competitors beat us on price they will eventually get our business. So we need to be efficient so we can keep our prices competitive.
Extend lean manufacturing ideas to nonmanufacturing workers to cut costs.	
Expand capacity.	One part of being efficient is having scale, or size. That allows us to spread our costs over more operations. It also improves our purchasing power—if we buy more we can get better prices from our suppliers. Achieving $5.5 billion in sales will keep us among the top three in size in our industry. That's where we need to be.
Grow geographically.	
Add new customers.	
Introduce new product lines to existing customers.	
Shift the product mix for builders in key markets.	
Add new product lines.	We can get size by getting more customers and selling more to them, but that alone won't get us to where we need to be. So to do that we will acquire companies.
Acquire companies in new areas with customers we don't have.	
Monitor a small set of key metrics and connect them to performance management and bonuses.	All of these factors are considered in the metrics we've established for the business. If we achieve each of those, we'll get to where we need to be.

Table 4.1.   **Bringing the Know into the Equation.**

THE LAND OF OZ KNOWS

Leadership at the Land of Oz, the company we introduced in Chapter Three, set goals of $5.5 billion and a 17-percent ROA. They identified a set of strategies that would achieve those goals. They then described in simple terms why those goals and those strategies made sense. Certainly, a driving factor behind their decisions was building shareholder value, which they did not ignore. They also related goals and strategies to competitive factors and trends in the industry. Although the underlying drivers behind strategy might have been complex, the leaders reduced them to very simple terms every employee could understand as illustrated in Table 4.1.

When combined with the information developed in determining the *Do* in the Action Equation, the *Know* provides a strong foundation for leadership communication about strategy. It's an explanation employees understood and accepted.

SUMMARY

Ensuring that employees know what they are supposed to do is an essential role of leadership communication. If leaders communicate this alone, they will be ahead of many companies. But there's more to leadership communication than that. Employees need to know the reasons behind goals and strategies. Answering their "why" questions helps reduce the distractions caused when they try to figure it out themselves—and we guarantee they will try. Employees want to understand not only why certain strategies were chosen by leadership and how those strategies are intended to benefit the business, but also how execution against the strategies will benefit them personally—the eternal "What's in it for me?" The reasons could be financial requirements, competitive factors, societal issues, industry trends, or customer trends. Relevant answers to the "why" questions can build confidence in leadership in the minds of employees and give a context to strategy that helps employees make decisions and trade-offs when they're needed.

Who needs to know the strategy? That's easy. Every leader in an organization should know the organization's strategy. In addition, certain groups of employees have a disproportionate impact on the execution of certain strategies, and leaders must consider this as they communicate. Some people need to know more detail than others.

Research and development people, for example, have a significant impact on strategies involving innovation and product leadership. Employees in manufacturing have a significant impact on quality and cost strategies. Leaders must consider this in developing their communication to ensure that specific groups have the opportunity to understand strategy at the level appropriate for their roles. Conversations about strategy among leaders and employees not only help the employees be more effective in their jobs, but also bring insight and information on strategy and its execution to leaders.

CHAPTER FIVE

Feel: What Do Employees Need to Feel to Take Action?

"These new routes will give us the geographic coverage we need to fuel growth, increase market share, and deliver higher returns to our shareholders." The airline CEO was addressing a group of employees, trying to gain their support for a controversial new acquisition. They responded with silence and an occasional smirk. You might have had a similar response, given the circumstances.

The airline's employees didn't want to go there. For them, the acquisition meant lost seniority and greater competition for the best assignments. Moreover, the employees hated the airline that the CEO intended to acquire. After years of talking about that competitor as the dregs of the industry, it was unthinkable to contemplate working side by side with its employees (let alone giving up your seat to one of them as well).

After this less-than-stellar start, the CEO changed his message. He shifted from a rational explanation of why the acquisition made sense to an emotional appeal. In essence, he said, "This acquisition will establish us once again in our rightful position as the most elite airline in the industry. That's who we are. That's what we deserve. We need to do what's necessary to make it happen." Within six weeks, a majority of employees were on the road to not only accepting the acquisition, but also supporting it. "This might be hard to swallow," they said. "But it will be worth the gulp."

The CEO won support for his strategy because he connected it to a destination that was important to employees—the feeling associated with being elite. Most of the employees loved their company (although they didn't care for management). They were proud of the airline's history and its long-time premier status in the industry. It gave them bragging rights to anybody who would listen. Indeed, they wore their elitism on their sleeves. Boasted one employee, "I fly to Paris once a month to visit a shop on the Champs Elysées to buy my favorite soap. I like to tell that to people at cocktail parties." Another said, "It's one thing to work in the airline business—like at Southwest. It's another thing to work at an airline that caters to CEOs, celebrities, and the international jet set. I've rubbed elbows with everybody from Bill Gates to Tom Cruise to Michael Jordan."

This elite position was where employees wanted to be. The merger was one of the key building blocks in the strategy of *how* the airline was going to get there. Business reality forced the acquisition: it was the only way the airline could get the routes it needed to grow. Employees, though, looked at the acquisition through a different lens. It was palatable because it provided a way the airline could regain the elite status they valued so much. When management framed the opportunity in terms that reached not only their heads but also their hearts, employees began to listen.

Information creates understanding; emotion drives action. People work for a paycheck; they die for a cause. People will show up and give some reasonable level of effort to get paid (and perhaps a bit more to get paid more), to have a sense of job security and opportunity, to avoid getting fired or criticized for poor performance and

> *There are intrinsic motivations in every work situation. Find and leverage them.*

the like. Effective leaders go beyond these rational motivations to create an emotional connection to the work they want employees to do—the *Feel* part of the Action Equation. They give meaning to work, to reach the deeper levels of motivation that drive the kind of action that separates high-performing organizations from the rest.

A study published in 1999 by Kenneth Kovach of George Mason University confirmed the power of emotion to affect employee behavior. In that study, he asked a thousand employees and one hundred of their bosses to list the things that they believe motivate employees.[1] Employees ranked factors such as participating in interesting work, feeling appreciated at work, and "being in on things" high on their lists. They ranked job security and good wages as important but lower on the list. Bosses, on the other hand, thought employees would be motivated by good wages and job security.

This discrepancy is nothing new. Back in 1959 Frederick Herzberg, the late professor of management and psychology, distinguished between "hygiene" factors and true motivators. Hygiene factors are the external elements that affect staff, including supervision, policies, working conditions, salary, and security. Motivators, on the other hand, are the intrinsic elements that affect staff, such as achievement, recognition, growth, responsibility, and the work itself. Herzberg found that the hygiene issues do not actually motivate staff, but are necessary to prevent dissatisfaction. The motivators inspire employees to improve their level of performance.[2]

On Strategy communication can be instrumental in tapping into the intrinsic motivations that make employees tick and are therefore essential to strategy execution and achieving results. Identifying and leveraging what's emotionally meaningful to employees requires a leader to think beyond business as usual. Achieving "bold goals" may be nirvana to a CEO, but it's often just a bunch

> *Leaders must find out where objectives and strategies intersect with employee motivations.*

of numbers to employees. Strategies revolving around acquisitions, a new sales model, or other business imperatives may be important to the company but not that compelling to employees. To motivate employees to the highest levels of action, a leader must find out where company objectives and strategies intersect with employee emotions. Note that these motivations don't necessarily reflect what management *wants* employees to care about; rather, what *actually* motivates employees intrinsically.

In our work with many different companies, we've encountered a number of motivational triggers that surface repeatedly. There are certainly others, but the following list provides a good starting point in identifying what motivates different employees in most companies.

- *The company's purpose.* These employees connect to what a company does—in effect, saying, "I'm here because our company does something special."

- *The company's products.* The product is king for these employees. Their feeling is, "I love the products—that's what I get up for in the morning."

- *The customer.* These employees have a special connection to the customer. "I'm here for *them,*" they might say.

- *The company's stature.* These employees are motivated by what being at their company says about them: "My company makes me special."

- *Their team.* This could be their immediate team, but they often connect to the larger company as "their" team as well. These employees feel, "I'm here for my mates. I'll do whatever I need to for them."

- *Their contribution.* The opportunity to contribute their skills is the key motivational connection for some employees. Their feeling is, "I'm here because I have the opportunity to contribute what I have to offer."

- *The substance of the work.* The work itself is the turn-on for many employees. These employees might say, "I'm here because I get to do the coolest work." We actually heard one employee at a technology consulting firm say, "We got to work on the Internet before it was the Internet. There aren't many places that could give me that kind of opportunity."

- *The accomplishment.* These employees like the feeling of collective accomplishment: "We get things done here. It feels good."

- *The sense of belonging.* "I feel comfortable here. I'm at home."

- *Contribution to community.* This motivation is similar to the connection to the company's purpose, but its focus is on community. These employees might say, "We're making the world (or our neighborhood) a better place."

When leaders consider these motivations, it changes the tone and content of their communication. For example, we worked with one company whose leaders continually emphasized customers in their communication. To improve customer service, their mantra was, "We need to do this for our customers. The customer is king." In reality, the employees didn't really care that much about customers; they cared about the substance of the work. "I'd do this even if they didn't pay me," said one employee. When asked whether the customer figured into his motivations, he said, "No. I do it because of the intellectual challenge involved. I love figuring out problems. It doesn't matter to me whether I do it for customers, or my boss, or my aunt in Minnesota."

The customer is often the default focus of leadership communication, and sometimes it's the right one. But often the intrinsic motivation of employees is something quite different. In this example, instead of saying "The customer is king," leadership should have said something like, "We are about innovative solutions that work. And they work only if customers are happy." That's one way you can connect employee motivation—the substance of the work—with leadership's strategy around customer satisfaction.

Sometimes what really motivates employees is different from what management would like it to be.

The motivational connections employees have with their company generally apply to the entire employee group of a company, if the experiences of those employees are similar. This is true in companies that have grown organically over time. Companies that have grown through acquisition, however, may include employees with very different motivational connections. For example, a technology company we worked with had acquired a smaller firm that operated in the same industry, doing an extension of the same work. However, the difference between the motivational connections in the two employee groups couldn't have been greater. Employees at the acquired company were in love with the substance of the work and what they could do for customers. Employees at the acquiring company, however, seldom mentioned the customer as they talked about what motivated them about work, and few employees cared about technology at all. They were there to sell, build business, and get ahead. If leadership hadn't recognized this difference at the outset and throughout the acquisition integration process, they easily could have alienated the new employees and destroyed the value of the company they had bought.

BE AN ORGANIZATIONAL PSYCHOLOGIST

A psychologist explores the inner workings of a person's emotional psyche. A leader must do the same thing concerning his or her organization to find out what really makes people tick. Often, when we suggest this to business leaders we get the "this is soft and fuzzy" eye roll—the sarcastic look that says this isn't really business. Many leaders don't like to talk about employee emotion, and they don't like to spend time or money on it. Moreover, even if they accept emotion as a legitimate leadership concern, many managers think they know what makes their employees tick, so they don't do the homework necessary to know for certain.

First, emotional communication is anything but soft and fuzzy. Take the Marines (and for that matter every branch of the military). As a matter of doctrine, they build in their "employees" an emotional commitment to their teams—the frontline squads that form the backbone of the fighting force. From the time a Marine first puts on a uniform, his or her drill sergeant begins to instill that commitment to team, along with other emotional connections to the organization such as pride in the Corps and elitism. That commitment goes well beyond the "rational" reasons why a soldier should walk into harm's way—to achieve mission objectives, to protect the country, and others. Actually, the fundamental reason men and women risk their lives in battle is because of the men and women that surround them. They do it for each other, for the team. If emotion isn't soft and fuzzy to the Marines, surely every business leader can embrace emotion as a legitimate part of leadership communication.

Employees' emotional connections to work and company are anything but "soft and fuzzy." They drive action that gets results.

Moreover, the process of identifying and leveraging employee emotion isn't soft and fuzzy either. Employee emotion can be identified, influenced, and measured just like productivity, quality, and cost. Marketers—and for that matter, politicians—live and die by the processes they use to identify customer and voter emotions, as well as the numbers they track about them. The same is true for employee emotions and leadership communication. We often track what employees *know* by asking them if they understand goals, objectives, and strategies. The same should be true concerning employee motivational connections.

Finally, when we talk about embracing emotion and suggest becoming an organizational psychologist, we don't mean you should be a pop psychologist or cheerleader. If leaders believe that employees will be motivated simply by clever sayings and posters, they will be disappointed. And if leaders believe they can get up in front of an audience of employees and cheer them on with a song-and-dance routine that isn't backed up by concrete communication and action, they will fail in embarrassing fashion. Take emotion seriously, and do the homework necessary to make it an effective part of On Strategy leadership communication.

GETTING THE INSIGHTS YOU NEED

Developing On Strategy communication, which includes identifying employee motivational connections, requires listening to employees in a way many leaders don't regularly do. In large, complex organizations, real listening requires some level of formality or process to ensure that the information uncovered is valid. Leaders also must listen at various levels, silos, and other subgroups within the organization to make sure all are represented as communication is developed.

The employee surveys most companies use don't provide much insight into employee motivational connections to the company and work. It takes a survey specifically designed for that purpose to uncover motivational insights. We're most familiar with the product provided by Senn Delaney Leadership, a leadership consulting firm, and have used their approach in our work. The research is quantitative, so it provides an excellent snapshot of the entire organization and also differentiates among various employee groups and levels. This is particularly helpful for organizations that may have multiple motivational connections (sort of like multiple personalities)—a situation that, again, is often the case when acquisitions are part of the equation. In addition, the quantitative research provides an excellent benchmark that helps evaluate progress and shifts in employee motivations.

However, formal research can take time and can be expensive. As an alternative, we've found qualitative research to be effective in identifying employee motivational connections. Discussion groups held with employees can identify motivations as well as other issues that affect On Strategy communication. Moreover, the qualitative research can be conducted quickly and primarily with internal resources. Guidance on how to create and facilitate effective employee discussion groups is in the "How to" Resource Guide (Chapter Twelve) at the end of this book.

Now let's see what the leaders of the Land of Oz found when they began exploring the intrinsic motivations of their employees.

THE LAND OF OZ GETS EMOTIONAL

At the Land of Oz—the company we have used as an ongoing case—we held an extensive discussion with the leadership team about their motivational connections, and we tested their feelings with those deeper in the organization. As is true in most cases, the connection was consistent.

Employees at the Land of Oz connected to their company through a sense of belonging. They felt they had "found a home." That sense of belonging was rooted in specific experiences in which the company and its leadership offered employees opportunity where little existed. For some, geography limited their opportunity. The company was located in a small town and there weren't many options. For others, leadership offered opportunities unavailable elsewhere because of a lack of education or experience, or other personal factors. The senior legal counsel, for example, had joined the company without a college degree. While at the company, he went to night school to earn a bachelor's degree and later a law degree. He was a self-starter, and the company had supported him every step of the way. When we talked with people deeper in the organization, the same kind of stories dominated discussions about what made the company special to them. They all had a story about how leadership at the company invited them to join and encouraged them to take advantage of opportunities. This became the collective experience of employees across the organization and, in essence, the dominant motivational connection. It was as if employees said, "The company opened its arms to me and enabled me to fulfill my aspirations."

This connection became very important for leaders to recognize. The company was undergoing exceptional growth, primarily through acquisitions. Growth could become a threat to employees if it appeared they were going to lose opportunities because of the influx of new employees, or if leadership became much less accessible. This fear was being exacerbated by the fact that the headquarters had outgrown its original building and employees were now spread over several locations. The company's acquisition spree also created fears that the company itself would be acquired. Stories of industry consolidation filled the newspapers. This was particularly troubling to this employee group. If another company purchased their "home," they believed it would certainly change for the worse.

Recognizing these insights, leadership was better prepared to communicate to employees. They could show that strategy execution would make their company stronger, create more opportunities, and protect the emotion that employees had invested in their company. The motivational connection informed the Action Equation (*Know + Feel = Do*) by filling in what employees needed to feel in order to support strategy: a sense of belonging—that they had found a home—and a belief that the company valued self-starters and provided them with opportunities unavailable elsewhere. At the Land of Oz, therefore, the Action Equation unfolded as depicted in Table 5.1.

SUMMARY

The rational elements of leadership communication are just one piece of the puzzle. Truly effective leaders also seek to understand and leverage the intrinsic emotional connections employees have with the company and their work. People will work for a paycheck, but they'll die for a cause—and every organization can find a cause. Nearly every job—even assembly line work and flipping burgers at a fast-food restaurant—has a motivational connection to employees. It might involve being part of a team, making cool products, or saving lives, but *something* can motivate an employee to do more than just clock in. It's a leader's job to find out what that is and tap into it by connecting strategy execution to that intrinsic motivation. That intersection between strategy and employee motivation is a key to performance. Communication can leverage it to drive results.

Do	Know	Feel
17% ROA	Know what to do, plus why.	A sense of belonging—that employees have found a home—and a belief that the company values self-starters and provides them with opportunities unavailable elsewhere.
$5.5 billion in sales	The company needs to achieve the scale necessary to maintain a low cost structure, and to take on competitors. Achieving these financial targets will accumulate the cash necessary to fund the work we need to do to grow, as well as to provide an appropriate return to shareholders, which is an obligation we have to them.	
Maintain high levels of customer satisfaction		
Implement lean manufacturing systems		
Introduce new training that focuses on cost reduction		
Trim non-value-add staff	We are in a commodity-type business—if competitors beat us on price they will eventually get our business. So we need to be efficient so we can keep our prices competitive.	
Extend lean manufacturing ideas to non-manufacturing workers to cut costs		
Expand capacity	One part of being efficient is having scale, or size. That allows us to spread our costs over more operations. It also improves our purchasing power—if we buy more we can get better prices from our suppliers. Achieving $5.5 billion in sales will keep us among the top three in size in our industry. That's where we have to be.	
Grow geographically		
Add new customers		
Introduce new product lines to existing customers		
Shift the product mix for builders in key markets	We can get size by getting more customers and selling more to them, but that alone won't get us to where we need to be. So, to do that we will acquire companies.	
Add new product lines		
Acquire companies in new areas with customers we don't have		
Monitor a small set of key metrics and connect them to performance management and bonuses	All of these factors are considered in the seven metrics we've established for the business. If we achieve each of those, we'll get to where we need to be.	

Table 5.1.   Bringing the Feel into the Equation.

CHAPTER SIX

The "Why Nots": What's Getting in the Way?

J ust as people do things for a reason, there are reasons why they *won't* do certain things.

"We're paying them. We're training them. We're giving them all the support they need. Why won't they make it happen?" That's what a frustrated division president said about his sales organization when his "value pricing" strategy began to falter. The strategy called for sales people to sell product on its lifetime value rather than its initial price, and it seemed to have everything going for it. It made good business sense because the product cost less for customers to operate over time, which justified a higher price at the outset. Leadership aligned compensation behind the strategy, paying much higher commissions on value-based sales. They trained the sales force in every facet of the concept and provided a high-tech tool that calculated the lifecycle value benefit for each customer based on their product usage. And finally, the strategy appealed to a key employee motivational trigger: pride in the product and how it served customers. Despite this, the new value-pricing strategy couldn't get off the ground.

There was something getting in the way, and leadership held a series of discussion groups to find out what it was. They discovered that sales people thought the concept had merit—it was good for customers. They also wanted the commissions and loved the training. But they didn't believe customers would actually buy product at a higher price. Their experience in the industry was that everybody sold on price. Even worse, the sales people didn't believe management would follow through and stick to the strategy. Over the years, they had been burned by a "program du jour" approach; they had seen new programs, incentives, and other initiatives come and go. They didn't want to be burned again, so they nodded affirmatively in meetings where leadership discussed the new value-pricing strategy, but out in the field they sold on price.

THE BEHAVIOR CHAIN

The sales force's actions were a result of what we call the Behavior Chain (see Figure 6.1). The Behavior Chain begins with a person's experiences, which shape their beliefs, which shape their behaviors, which drive results. Leadership must consider the Behavior Chain in developing On Strategy communication. It provides the insights necessary to address the reasons why people don't take action—the "why nots."

Figure 6.1.   The Behavior Chain.

In our work, we've encountered a number of "why nots" revealed through analysis of the Behavior Chain. Employees cite experiences that shape beliefs that make it difficult for them to change their behavior in order to follow leadership's direction to management. Some prevalent beliefs are as follows:

"This will pass, just like the last program of the month." We hear a lot of that, just as we did in the opening example. It strikes at employee confidence in management's commitment to strategy. Because of past experiences, they don't believe they can trust that leadership will follow through with plans and strategies, and they fear they will be left holding the bag. This belief blocks leadership's attempts to drive new behaviors, as employees continue past practices while waiting for new strategies to die on the vine.

"They lied to us." We hear this a lot too. It involves leadership candor and motives. It's an experience, either real or perceived, that leadership isn't telling the truth, or that there are ulterior motives behind leadership's words. Management at one company, for example, needed greater efficiency from one of its production facilities and approached employees and their union with work rule changes. Employees would hear none of it because they said management had misled them in the last negotiation. Management replied, "We did not lie." We looked at their statements, and it was true: management had not lied in the literal sense. However, they had communicated in terms so convoluted and full of babble that employees could not see the truth. Many believed that was management's intent. "If they weren't trying to cover something up," one employee said, "why would we need a lawyer to figure out what they were talking about?"

"They didn't ask me, so why would it work?" This is what employees often say about strategies developed for their work areas without their input. Experience tells them that the programs don't work well (or at least employees think they don't) when they have not been involved in developing them. Even if they might work, employees often undermine them because they were not included in the process, and the expectation of failure becomes a self-fulfilling prophecy. The lack of inclusion fuels two sets of beliefs: (1) management doesn't care what employees think, and (2) management didn't do the homework to make sure the new way of doing things would really work. Both beliefs lead to the same behavior—resistance—and the same result: poor strategy execution.

We witnessed this "why not" in action recently when we were checking into one of the airline clubs at the airport. The receptionist typed into her computer, shook her head, typed more into her computer, and grumbled, "The kid with the MBA who put this new system together was an idiot. They never asked us a thing, and it doesn't work. It will take a minute for me to get around it." Whatever the kid with the MBA was thinking he was going to accomplish with the new system was erased, along with our confidence as customers that the company was going to get its act together. The system was a victim of the "work-around"—the common practice of employees trying hard to get their jobs done by working around the new systems and processes installed by management.

Employee experiences with management and the company lead to "why nots"—reasons why they won't deliver the behavior leadership needs.

"*It's not me, it's the worker behind the tree.*" The blame game is a common reason for inaction. Employees complain they can't get anything done because other departments or silos block their progress. The experiences associated with this "why not" are rooted in company bureaucracy and politics; in unclear roles, responsibilities, and accountabilities; and in a lack of cross-functional communication. Employees really believe they can't get anything done, and they really believe nothing will happen to them if they don't. We often see this "why not" in matrix organizations, as well as in organizations in which one function dominates the others. Leadership at one company, for example, wanted product development engineers to be more aggressive in driving quality in manufacturing, which reported up to a different silo. At one point, manufacturing even violated the safety standards of a product to reduce production costs, while engineers stood by and watched. "That's manufacturing's job," they said—and they resisted greater involvement and accountability. Likewise, manufacturing managers said, "Engineering is responsible for product design. If they didn't like what we wanted to do, they should have said something." This "why not" was rooted in a long history of functional rivalry that inhibited cooperation, in addition to a lack of leadership clarity about roles and responsibilities. Employees believed that challenging a sister function was the quickest way to the doghouse, and nobody took ownership of critical quality issues.

"You're out-voted." This "why not" quashes alternative thinking that challenges the predominant view in an organization, and it leads to stale performance or costly mistakes. In some organizations, employees categorize people into the "in group" and the "out group" (although they may not use these high-schoolish terms). Individuals in the in group get so comfortable with their collective view that they will preserve this unanimity at all cost. They will get people to buy into group loyalty and establish implicit agreements to not bring up upsetting facts. This leads to groupthink. In this situation, the group is so concerned with maintaining unanimity that they fail to evaluate all their alternatives and options and sometimes ignore crucial information. As a result, they don't raise difficult issues or question weak arguments, and strategy isn't subject to the critical due diligence that's needed to develop effective direction and manage implementation.

For a truck manufacturer we worked with, groupthink stifled innovative discussion. In one exchange we witnessed, for example, an executive new to the company and the industry questioned the wisdom of continuing to build products that consistently resulted in a financial loss for the business. In response, a long-time executive mentioned it wouldn't be "truck smart" to discontinue the products. That was shorthand for telling the new executive that he was challenging views long held by the group, and that wasn't acceptable. The new executive responded, "I didn't know you had to be business stupid to be truck smart." Things didn't go well after that.

"Why take the risk?" We often hear leaders implore their employees to "take reasonable risks." Employees nod, but this "why not" is their unspoken response. They then take the route of least risk as they try to achieve their objectives. Innovation and creativity suffer, as do results. That's often the direct result of leadership actions that first ask for risk taking, but then dress down, demote, or fire people for failure.

The "why nots" extend beyond this short list. Before taking action, employees also ask themselves questions such as "Will pursuing this course of action or sharing this information hurt my career? Embarrass me? Hurt my peers and therefore my relationship with them? Invite retaliation? Make me look adversarial? Make it look like I don't have a positive, can-do attitude?" Employee experiences with the company and management answer these questions and drive behavior. The lesson here is that leaders must try to understand why employees don't act by examining the root causes of behavior—the experiences and beliefs of the Behavior Chain—and addressing them at their source. Over the long term, this saves time and resources and prevents costly mistakes.

ADDRESSING A "WHY NOT"

Leaders usually can't simply talk "why nots" away. These objections often are too ingrained in the organization or too powerfully burned into the employee mindset to be overcome with information alone. Because "why nots" are rooted in experience, leaders must overcome them by creating a new experience that is unambiguously contrasted, and equal in magnitude, with the prior experience that shaped employee beliefs. It's similar to the technique some psychologists use to relieve their patients of certain phobias. They overcome a fear of flying, for example, with a series of structured, supported flying experiences. Depending on the source and depth of the fear, more or fewer positive experiences are required to overcome it.

If employees believe management has lied to them, management must prove they tell the truth. Simply saying "I tell the truth" won't do it (Richard Nixon's famous declaration "I am not a crook" didn't make his problems go away, although it helps if the declaration is true). To build trust, leaders must create a deliberate process whereby they say to employees what they are going to do, do it, and then remind employees that they did what they said they would do.

> *Leaders can't simply talk "why nots" away. They must create a new experience that drives new beliefs.*

Moreover, this process must be very visible—telling the truth where nobody hears or sees it won't move the dial.

If employees believe leadership doesn't involve them in decision making and therefore doesn't make good decisions, leadership must implement a very visible process for employee involvement. Again, a speech won't do it. Putting a suggestion box in the lunchroom, creating quality circles, holding a meeting to voice employee ideas are all reasonable starting points to the process. They are meaningless, however, until leadership takes action on employee input and communicates that action to employees so they connect it to the suggestions they have made. That creates the new experience, which leads to a new belief, which will drive new behaviors.

If groupthink suppresses dissenting opinions and then destroys managers who buck the majority, merely conducting a workshop promoting the value of diverse thinking won't solve the problem. Leaders must both recognize and reward people who challenge the group and punish managers who stifle dissent. It has to be more than words in a speech or training—it has to be real. The new experience must be commensurate in intensity and duration to fully overcome the previous experience. And it must be very visible.

In the case of the uncooperative sales group, experience was the root cause of their inaction. The company's initial approach to engaging them in a new behavior—selling on value instead of price— involved changing compensation and training. Although important, these didn't strike directly at the "why not" reasons why the sales people didn't support the strategy: issues around confidence and their belief in leadership's commitment. To address the problem, leaders had to start with the root causes—the experiences the sales people had in the field and management's tendency to abandon new initiatives (see Figure 6.2).

To turn this situation around and get the behaviors they needed, leadership created a new experience designed to drive a new belief— that customers are willing to listen and buy based on value, and that management was sticking to this strategy no matter what. The division president held "president's dinners" in key markets across the country to show his commitment to the program and put *his* reputation on the line with customers before he asked sales people to risk their relationships. How often do you see that?

At the dinners, which top sales people attended along with potential customers, the president made a presentation to customers and led a discussion about the new products and the lifetime value concept. It showed the sales people that leadership was serious and committed and wasn't going to leave the sales people hanging. It also demonstrated that the value-pricing approach worked. The substantial sales resulting from the presentations showed that the right customers would respond positively to the new product and marketing approach. Following the dinners, the word spread among the sales force, and the value-pricing strategy had new legs.

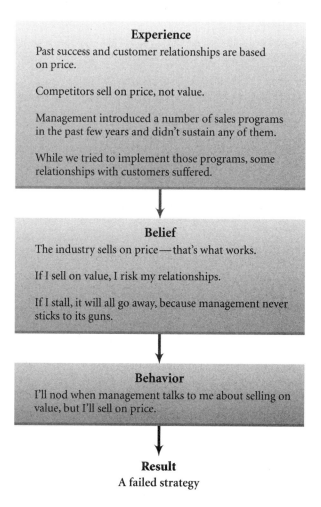

Experience

Past success and customer relationships are based on price.

Competitors sell on price, not value.

Management introduced a number of sales programs in the past few years and didn't sustain any of them.

While we tried to implement those programs, some relationships with customers suffered.

Belief

The industry sells on price—that's what works.

If I sell on value, I risk my relationships.

If I stall, it will all go away, because management never sticks to its guns.

Behavior

I'll nod when management talks to me about selling on value, but I'll sell on price.

Result

A failed strategy

Figure 6.2.   The Behavior Chain: The Way It Is.

The strategy would have failed before it started without the aggressive leadership communication displayed by the president of the division. The communication created a new experience for the sales force, which overcame the past and created new beliefs around management and their strategies. That doesn't mean the company's moves to promote the new strategy, change compensation, and train the sales force were off target—each of those steps was important to driving strategy execution—but they were ineffective until

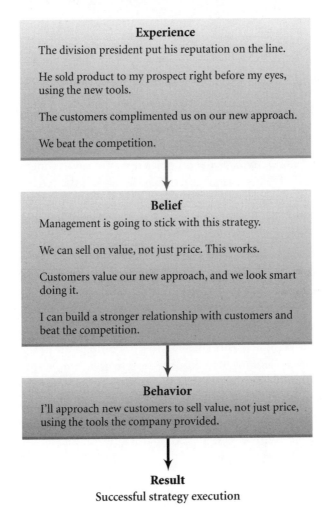

Experience
The division president put his reputation on the line.

He sold product to my prospect right before my eyes, using the new tools.

The customers complimented us on our new approach.

We beat the competition.

Belief
Management is going to stick with this strategy.

We can sell on value, not just price. This works.

Customers value our new approach, and we look smart doing it.

I can build a stronger relationship with customers and beat the competition.

Behavior
I'll approach new customers to sell value, not just price, using the tools the company provided.

Result
Successful strategy execution

Figure 6.3. The Behavior Chain: The Way You Want to See It.

leadership addressed the root causes of employee behavior and addressed the "why nots" (see Figure 6.3).

BE AN ORGANIZATIONAL ARCHEOLOGIST

The "why nots" are usually found in a company's history. And just as an archeologist digs up the secrets of past civilizations, leaders must dig up the experiences that have shaped employee beliefs. In this role, there are a number of places a leader can look to uncover the "why nots."

Most companies have an employee survey, although these differ greatly in purpose and content. To inform leadership communication, study the research to identify responses that relate to what employees know and feel—and an indication of a "why not"—such as questions/statements about the following issues:

- *Confidence in management.* Look for responses to statements such as "I believe management has a well-formulated business strategy for the present," "I believe management has a clear vision for the future," and "I have confidence in the future of the company."

- *Trust and candor.* These include statements such as "In our company, even difficult issues are discussed with tact and insight," "In our company, communication between leaders and their direct reports is candid and productive," and "I trust management to tell the truth."

- *Teamwork.* Statements such as "In our company, it is easy for us to combine and evaluate information from multiple sources," "In our company, all employees are committed to doing quality work," and "I have a best friend at work."

- *Participation.* These include "Management trusts the judgment of people at my level in the company" and "Sufficient effort is made to get the opinions and thinking of employees in this company."

- *Motives.* "In my company, we discuss even the most difficult issues with tact and insight."

- *Accountability.* "I understand how my work contributes to the company's business objectives."

- *Direction.* "Management has a clear view of where the organization is going and how to get there" and "I understand leadership's vision for the company."

- *Commitment.* "Management delivers on its promises" and "Management's actions match its words."

As you interpret the impact of survey questions, it's helpful to break down results into subsets involving specific parts and levels of the organization. This will help set priorities for your leadership communication. For example, if a function or division is especially critical to hitting your objectives, you

Look to the company's history, and the stories employees tell, to identify the "why nots."

will want to look more closely at that subset to determine how leadership communication can drive performance in that specific area.

It's important that you as a leader consider the implications of research data as it relates to your company, not to the industry norms. Even if your company scores well compared with your peers, for example, that could be misleading. Being in the top tier of a dysfunctional group shouldn't be comforting (any more than being the sanest person in the sanitarium). Likewise, if one quarter of your employees don't believe in your strategy, it is important to understand who those employees are. If they are people, such as the janitorial staff and others who have little or no impact on your strategy, there's less reason to lose sleep over it. But if the scores are low among the people who can affect strategy execution, then it's a problem.

Review of formal research usually can provide a place to begin exploring the root causes of "why nots" and can help prioritize leadership's focus. A deeper look into the organization is usually required, however, to truly understand the Behavior Chain. Although formal research points leaders in the right direction, interactive listening and conversations with employees provide the depth of understanding and the concrete examples needed to address issues.

Employee discussion groups can be a very effective tool for understanding the Behavior Chain. Specifically, the questions in a discussion group designed to inform a Behavior Chain seek to understand what tangible experiences employees have been through or live in the lore of the organization that shape their beliefs on a particular subject. Questions such as "When you have done what management has asked in the past, what has happened?" and "When you have a really tough, frustrating day, what does it look like?" and "What makes working here hard?" elicit answers that give leaders tremendous insight into what kinds of experiences and feelings may be preventing action on the part of employees. With that knowledge, leaders are far better prepared to remove barriers to action.

(The review of discussion groups in the "How to" Resource Guide, Chapter Twelve, offers an overview of this technique for having conversations with employees.)

THE LAND OF OZ CONFRONTS ITS DEMONS

The Land of Oz, the company we've used to illustrate the *Know* + *Feel* = *Do* Action Equation, faced a few "why nots." Leadership had identified customer satisfaction as one of its nonnegotiables. They also wanted to institute more uniform processes and systems through a lean manufacturing approach that every operation would adopt. Employees' experiences, however, had led them to believe that volume would trump quality every time, even if it resulted in customer protests. Moreover, the company had always focused on cost—in fact, cost and volume were the primary means by which management evaluated line managers. At this company, employees believed they could survive anything but high costs. Moreover, the company had always operated in a very decentralized manner, and managers were given broad discretion on deciding how they would achieve their results. Managers knew the best way to move up in the organization was to demonstrate their ability to think independently, take action, and get results.

Leadership expected employees to make customer satisfaction a nonnegotiable and to embrace the uniform processes of its lean manufacturing approach. To drive behavior in these areas, leaders needed to address the Behavior Chain experiences that had created beliefs contrary to these strategies. They had to show that improving customer satisfaction, including quality, was a key ingredient in how employees would be evaluated. Moreover, manufacturing employees in particular needed to know that implementing lean manufacturing was the path to advancement at the company. Leadership communication in both instances would need to involve not only words, but also very visible actions.

With this understanding of the "why nots," leadership at the Land of Oz had a complete picture of the landscape in which they would conduct leadership communication on strategy. They were now ready to package this information for delivery to the organization, as shown in Table 6.1.

Table 6.1. Putting the Whole Equation Together.

Do	Know	Feel
17% ROA	Know what to do, plus why	A sense of belonging—that employees have found a home—and a belief that the company values self-starters and provides them with opportunities unavailable elsewhere
$5.5 billion in sales	The company needs to achieve the scale necessary to maintain a low cost structure, and to take on competitors. Achieving these financial targets will accumulate the cash necessary to fund the work we need to do to grow, as well as to provide an appropriate return to shareholders, which is an obligation we have to them.	
Maintain high levels of customer satisfaction		
Implement lean manufacturing systems		
Introduce new training that focuses on cost reduction		
Trim non-value-add staff	We are in a commodity-type business—if competitors beat us on price they will eventually get our business. So we need to be efficient so we can keep our prices competitive.	
Extend lean manufacturing ideas to non-manufacturing workers to cut costs		
Expand capacity	One part of being efficient is having scale, or size. That allows us to spread our costs over more operations. It also improves our purchasing power—if we buy more we can get better prices from our suppliers. Achieving $5.5 billion in sales will keep us among the top three in size in our industry. That's where we have to be.	**"WHY NOTS"** Current beliefs: Cost is king, and volume comes before quality. Even if they talk about customer satisfaction, they worry most about cost. Distinguish yourself by thinking and acting independently. If you do what everybody else does, you are just part of the pack.
Grow geographically		
Add new customers		
Introduce new product lines to existing customers	We can get size by getting more customers and selling more to them, but that alone won't get us to where we need to be. So, to do that we will acquire companies.	
Shift the product mix for builders in key markets		
Add new product lines		
Acquire companies in new areas with customers we don't have		
Monitor a small set of key metrics and connect them to performance, management, and bonuses	All of these factors are considered in the seven metrics we've established for the business. If we achieve each of those, we'll get to where we need to be.	

SUMMARY

Just as there are reasons why employees will take action, there are reasons why they won't. These are the "why nots." They often involve deep emotions around employee perceptions of management regarding issues such as trust, commitment, and competency. "Why not" issues are a significant challenge to employee motivation and a barrier to strategy execution.

The "why nots" usually can't be talked away. When employees believe they have been lied to by management, for example, leadership can't simply say "Trust me" and expect employees to respond with the best behaviors. Instead, leaders must address the root cause of the belief, identifying the experiences that shaped the negative belief about trust. This connection between experiences, beliefs, and behaviors is called the Behavior Chain. Leaders can identify the links of the Behavior Chain and how they affect behavior and results by reviewing many of the responses on their employee surveys as well as by conducting qualitative research among employees, typically through discussion groups.

To reverse a "why not," leadership must address the experience link in the Behavior Chain. For example, to overcome the barrier of established mistrust, a leader might begin by telling employees that he or she will always tell the truth in a straightforward manner. Then the leader must prove it through visible, demonstrable actions—telling the truth about difficult subjects, for example. Finally, the leader must remind employees that he or she told the truth. This words-actions-words cycle creates a new experience for employees, which in turn shapes a new belief. After enough cycles of telling the truth (and reminding employees of it), employees will begin to trust leadership's words again.

Leaders have been successful using this approach to address a wide variety of "why nots." Removing the "why nots" as a factor in the minds of employees puts leaders firmly on the path to successful strategy execution.

CHAPTER SEVEN

Package: Turn the Action Equation into a Conversation

—⁓— "Finally, something from corporate that I can use." That's what we heard from supervisors headed to the plant floor to talk to their employees and take on the Teamsters Union. Their plant was in the midst of a heated union organization drive, and it wasn't looking good for the company. The Teamsters knew what they were doing. They attacked the company on a few key points, such as a recent increase in the employee co-pay for health insurance. The union also made promises that they couldn't keep—that a contract would provide employees with more security, better wages, and rules that would protect them from working too hard. The company's approach was to attack the union with hour-long presentations about wage differentials, the country's rising health care costs, the decline in the number of union jobs, and how management believed unions have screwed up the country. It all seemed to go in one ear and out the other, and managers and supervisors drifted to the sidelines of the overall communication effort.

But now the "suits" from corporate were offering a different approach. They provided a short communication platform for supervisors that made sense to them and was easy to remember. It related to what employees—including the supervisors themselves—valued in their jobs. Moreover, they quit using corporate language, and framed the messages in the vernacular of supervisors. Job "positions" became "spots." "Influence" became "we have a say." And "the positive impact of the company's operating approach" became "we've got a good thing going." The new message was something supervisors could talk to people about not only in conference rooms but also in the day-to-day conduct of their work, and something that would relate well to employees.

The suits didn't get to this point without contention. "Supervisors can't handle this. They aren't good at communication," said managers from across the plant. True, supervisors weren't good at communicating the messages leadership gave them. Those messages were long, detailed, and complex. Besides, the information they were asking the supervisors to deliver was just anti-union propaganda, and they couldn't talk about it with a straight face. The company was going to lose the vote, and that meant the plant manager was going to lose his job. He was ready to try something different. "This might be unconventional," he said. "But it makes sense."

He and his team worked with the suits to make the message relevant to employees and deliverable by managers and supervisors. They knew what they needed employees to do: vote no. And they worked through what employees would have to know, and then feel, in order to vote that way. They learned that the vote wasn't really about the union; it was about employees and what was important to them. They came to realize unions make sense in some plants, but not this one and not with these employees. They distilled their message into five simple concepts that told a story about the plant and its employees, and why staying union-free was the best decision.

When supervisors first saw the message they laughed—not because it was funny but because they saw that management finally got it. "This is about us," they said. "This is about what people are really thinking. This is the truth. We can talk to them about this." As one of the suits said, "This information will resonate with employees." The supervisors laughed at that too because it was so corporate. But the suit was right. The supervisors took the message to the plant floor, employees listened, and the company won the vote by a 3 to 1 margin. At the end of it all, a couple of supervisors presented the suits with T-shirts with the words "The Resonator" printed on the front—because, yes, simplicity and truth do resonate.

CONVERSATIONS ARE "IN THE MOMENT"

It would be great if all managers and supervisors took the time to read and memorize the lengthy documents leadership provides so they could communicate their content. In an ideal world, everyone would be a gifted communicator who easily translates complex concepts into everyday language. And employees would listen to all the communication leaders send and work to digest and interpret it.

In the real world, that's not how it works. People listen intermittently and only to what interests them most. Employee memories are short (except when it's about management mistakes). They discuss things in short conversations, not extended debates. They don't have the time. Managers and supervisors communicate well enough to do their day-to-day jobs, but complex messages and issues can tax their communication ability (in this they are just like anybody else—just watch the political debates to see even intensively trained and experienced communicators stumble when things get complex). People are comfortable with the vernacular they have devel-

Leaders must be prepared to communicate on strategy "in the moment" with employees.

oped over a lifetime, and we aren't going to change that. Words and actions don't always fit together naturally for many employees, especially in complicated business situations.

In reality, effective leaders communicate "in the moment" when employees are listening, and they have to deliver a message that makes sense quickly.

They must communicate not only in controlled meetings, but also anywhere employees are having conversations about work—on the plant floor, in the elevator, by the water cooler, in the parking lot on the way to their cars, at the local pub where people gather for a beer—everywhere.

That's a tall order. A critical step in the process is to give managers and supervisors "something we can use." The work done to inform the Action Equation is a great start. It identifies what employees need to do and what motivates them to take action. Then it has to be packaged in a way that is easily delivered, heard, and remembered by leader and employee alike.

THE MEMORY ISSUE

If leaders are to communicate to employees in the moment, they must be able to remember their message from the top of their minds, not from a binder or note pad or little card they carry in a pocket. Unfortunately, human memory isn't capable of what leaders often ask of it. Even the shortened direction developed to inform the Action Equation is too lengthy and complex for most people to communicate without further packaging. They just can't remember it.

Human short-term memory capacity is limited to about five "chunks" of information, according to research conducted as far back as 1956. Princeton Professor of Psychology George Miller conducted extensive testing of people and their ability to recall lists of digits, and found humans are able to recall between five and nine chunks of information.[1] So the fact that people can't remember all that much doesn't mean they are dimwits; it's biology. If leaders ask managers and supervisors to communicate more, they will exceed their capacity to remember the messages they are supposed to deliver. Moreover, the employees they are talking to will have trouble remembering the information, and communication really doesn't happen unless the receiver of the information hears it and retains it. If you believe we're underestimating you or the people who work with you, try the memory experiment we outline in the "How to" Resource Guide (Chapter Twelve) with a group of managers. It takes only five minutes and demonstrates just how limited human short-term memory is. Also, it's fun to watch super-smart engineers, financial wizards, and linguistic gymnasts (or so they think) struggle to remember a handful of words, as asked in the experiment.

Human memory capacity enables us to remember only about five chunks of information. That limits the message leaders can deliver.

To prepare leaders to communicate in the moment, we have to enable them to do it from memory. At the outset, that means using their short-term memory (over time, information will be committed to long-term memory, but that takes quite a bit of time, and it must be held in short-term memory first). That means communications must be limited to about five chunks of information. The chunks can be very large pieces of information, such as a movie passage or a piece of advertising, or a single fact. Also, the more the chunks of information relate to each other—as if held within a story—the easier it is for people to remember. These chunks can then be related to other, more detailed streams of information, as we'll outline later. But people won't get to that information unless they can use the five chunks as a guide or pathway to it. This five-chunk limit holds true for listeners as well as those who deliver the information. If you try to communicate a message that's too complex and lengthy, the people you are communicating to just won't remember it. More likely, they will remember what they want to hear, not what you say (and that causes all sorts of problems).

This limitation is particularly important to consider as messages move down the chain of command, through leaders to the field. A senior team that has developed strategy may be able to remember most of the elements of the Action Equation because they were deeply involved in developing it. The same won't be true for others. This is one reason management tends to believe supervisors aren't good at communication. We believe that's unfair to supervisors—and lets management off the hook. The real problem is that senior management gives supervisors material they can't communicate. In fact, the best communicators available—from Bill Clinton to Ronald Reagan—would have a hard time communicating the corporate-speak at many companies. And that means not just delivering a speech, but communicating in a way that employees understand and compels them to take action. Moreover, the environments in which supervisors communicate aren't like the quiet corners of the boardroom or front office. They are noisy, active locations bustling with activity. It's very difficult to remember complex points amidst distractions—especially when employees are firing questions at you. This makes communicating in the moment particularly challenging.

THE CONVERSATION PLATFORM

The Conversation Platform is a tool that helps leaders—from the CEO to frontline supervisors—remember the information they need to communicate so they can do so in the moment. It delivers information so employees will listen and can remember. It promotes conversations instead of presentations, speeches, and one-way monologues.

The Conversation Platform combines the most pertinent elements of the Action Equation into a simple, five-chunk message set.

The Conversation Platform is not a list of message points, however. Each of the five chunks is a conceptual gateway to all of the information in the Action Equation. The chunks are not phrases that tell the whole story, but concepts that represent the larger body of information, which embodies strategy, leadership's direction, or an organization's position on significant issues. At the same time, the Conversation Platform is a filter that helps leaders deliver On Strategy information and, likewise, eliminate babble from their leadership communication efforts. If information doesn't fit through the Platform's gateway, it's likely the information is off-strategy and irrelevant.

The Conversation Platform frames an organization's strategic messages in a way leaders can remember and talk about them and employees can hear them.

The Conversation Platform is composed of three parts. First is the core message, which may be about strategy or an issue; it is the central theme of the platform. It usually combines (1) the essence of what leadership wants employees to do with (2) the motivational connection that will make them want to take action—what we often call the "cause."

The second component of the Conversation Platform is a set of four building blocks that support the core message. They provide the actions that will deliver strategy, or the rationale that supports management's position on an issue. As appropriate, the building blocks also connect to the "whys" and "why nots" outlined in the Action Equation. Emphasis on the specific information depends on how relevant and important it is to driving employee actions and results. We restrict the building blocks to four, because when combined with the cause, the platform reaches our recommended limit of memory capacity: five chunks.

The third component of the Conversation Platform is supporting concepts and proof points that provide perspective and relate words with actions so they are connected and mutually supportive. Specific actions, budgets, projects, and resources provide proof points and show that the strategy that leaders are talking about is more than words. The proof points may also concern information that supports management's position on an issue.

The Conversation Platform does not necessarily include every piece of information in the Action Equation. Instead, it organizes the information to condense it and make it more accessible. It puts buckets of information into groupings so they are more memorable, and it organizes those buckets into a story in which all the parts relate to each other. This makes it not only easier for people to remember but also more appropriate for conversations. That's because people tend to have conversations around stories, not lists of activities.

The platform expresses *concepts* that leaders, and subsequently employees, put into their own words. It is not a collection of phrases, tag lines, slogans, or other sets of words that leaders memorize and repeat. The Conversation Platform focuses on the strength and clarity of concepts, not the ring of the words or cleverness of phrases. It is not a brochure, ad, video, or memo that is distributed. It's a leadership tool.

A leader can get started on developing a platform by using the simple five-box template depicted in Figure 7.1, which helps organize thinking and keep it short. (We recommend you print this template on one page and use at least 10-point type to fill in the building-block description in each box; this will help keep it short.) The center box holds the organization's purpose as expressed to employees. The other four boxes hold the building blocks. The five boxes should relate to each other so they tell a story. Infused

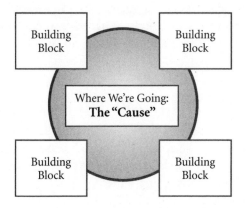

Figure 7.1. A Conversation Platform Template.

throughout are the reasons why the information is relevant to employees. This circular arrangement helps organize the information so managers can begin at any point in the story and segue into the other concepts as appropriate.

THE LAND OF OZ GETS READY TO ROLL

When leadership at the Land of Oz was ready to share the information that made up their Action Equation, they translated it into the five concept chunks of the Conversation Platform. Table 7.1 outlines the information employees needed to know and feel in order to achieve the company's goals, and how leadership "chunked" the information so it was easier for leaders and employees up and down the organization to remember.

Supervisors will remember the concepts and more, because the concepts lead to other information. The five concepts provide a way to organize and access the entire body of information informed by the Action Equation. Moreover, leaders still will need the background facts, supporting information, and perspective to add depth to the story, but all of that information must connect to the Conversation Platform. Table 7.2 shows how the concepts act as a summary and a gateway to other information that fits into the story.

In addition to relating all the Action Equation information to a simple set of statements employees can remember, all of the Conversation Platform elements connect the dots to form a story that can start from any of the boxes. For example, if an employee asks why the company is implementing lean manufacturing, the answer would be to increase efficiency so we can achieve a 17-percent ROA. That, in turn, is important to creating the capital the company needs to invest and grow, which is central to maintaining the opportunities for every employee.

WHEN ISSUES ARE THE ISSUE

In the union-organizing situation outlined earlier, the Conversation Platform took a somewhat different twist. It was more about an issue than specific strategies, and again front and center was the "cause": "We've got a good thing going—the best jobs in the county. We're the only ones who can keep it going" (see Figure 7.2). We based the core message of the platform on employees' belief that they had

Know + Feel		Chunked Message
17% ROA. $5.5 billion in sales. A sense of belonging—that they have found a home—and a belief that the company values self-starters and provides them with opportunities unavailable elsewhere.	The Cause	Achieve nothing less than a 17% ROA, while reaching $5.5 billion, to generate the capital we need to grow, and to keep the doors of opportunity open for all employees.
Implement lean manufacturing systems. Introduce new training that focuses on cost reduction. Trim non-value-add staff. Maintain high levels of customer satisfaction (the constant).	Building Block 1	Increase efficiency and reduce waste in everything we do by using new tools and focusing on what customers value.
Add new customers. Introduce new product lines to existing customers. Shift the product mix for builders in key markets. Add new product lines.	Building Block 2	Find new customers and sell more products and services to every customer.
Expand capacity. Grow geographically. Acquire companies in new areas with customers we don't have.	Building Block 3	Acquire and integrate new operations to extend our reach and coverage.
Measure success through a handful of key metrics that really count, including a new customer satisfaction measure.	Building Block 4	Measure success through a handful of key metrics that really count, including a new customer satisfaction measure.

Table 7.1. Translating the Action Equation into a Conversation Platform.

	Chunk	Connecting facts, concepts, and proof points
The Cause	Achieve nothing less than a 17% ROA, while reaching $5.5 billion, to generate the capital we need to grow, and to keep the doors of opportunity open for all employees.	Provides scale to be more competitive—we can't continue to be competitive in a consolidating industry without scale.
		The sales and return goals will provide the right amount of cash for acquisitions.
		Provides security, prevents us from being bought, and growth provides new opportunities.
Building Block 1	Increase efficiency and reduce waste in everything we do by using new tools and focusing on what customers value.	Commodity-type business demands efficiency.
		Competitors are becoming more efficient.
		Always keep the customer in mind (nonnegotiable).
		Use a suite of new tools: 5S, TPM, visual management, SMED, batch size reduction, cellular manufacturing, standardized work, work balancing, production leveling/smoothing, point-of-use systems, and so on.
		Offer training programs on these new tools.
		Use metrics: KPIs on accident frequency, on-time delivery, velocity of inventory; sales per employee; days payable outstanding; AR percent outstanding.

Building Block 2	Find new customers, and sell more products and services to every customer.	Some growth comes from existing customers, but we can't achieve our goals by this alone. Always keep the customer in mind (nonnegotiable). Add new product and distribution programs. Create special program for key, large customers to gain share. Convert customers to new product mix.
Building Block 3	Acquire and integrate new operations to extend our reach and coverage.	Acquire companies to achieve the scale. Scale makes us more competitive and secure; growth provides us with opportunity. Add new product lines in specialty areas. Add new industrial plants to leverage large customers. Pursue geographic expansion to key cities.
Building Block 4	Measure success through a handful of key metrics that really count, including a new customer satisfaction measure.	If we watch seven metrics together as a group, we'll get to our goals in the most efficient, effective way—and will remember to serve customers the right way: net sales, customer survey, safety, sales per employee, AR percent current, PBOP per employee, velocity of inventory.

Table 7.2. Connecting Proof Points to the Platform.

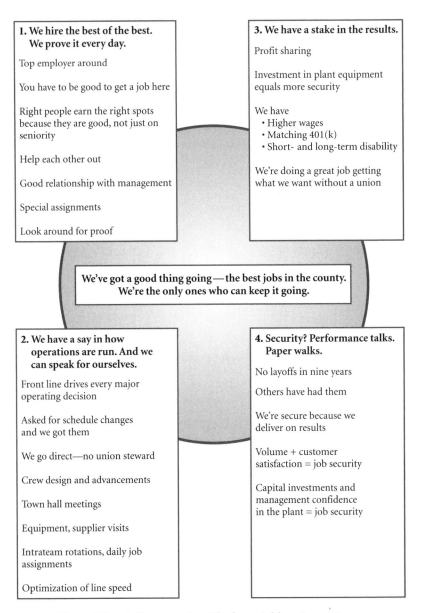

1. We hire the best of the best. We prove it every day.

Top employer around

You have to be good to get a job here

Right people earn the right spots because they are good, not just on seniority

Help each other out

Good relationship with management

Special assignments

Look around for proof

3. We have a stake in the results.

Profit sharing

Investment in plant equipment equals more security

We have
- Higher wages
- Matching 401(k)
- Short- and long-term disability

We're doing a great job getting what we want without a union

We've got a good thing going—the best jobs in the county. We're the only ones who can keep it going.

2. We have a say in how operations are run. And we can speak for ourselves.

Front line drives every major operating decision

Asked for schedule changes and we got them

We go direct—no union steward

Crew design and advancements

Town hall meetings

Equipment, supplier visits

Intrateam rotations, daily job assignments

Optimization of line speed

4. Security? Performance talks. Paper walks.

No layoffs in nine years

Others have had them

We're secure because we deliver on results

Volume + customer satisfaction = job security

Capital investments and management confidence in the plant = job security

Figure 7.2.   A Conversation Platform Addressing an Issue.

good jobs. It also spoke to a motivational connection the employees had that revolved around a strong sense of independence. These were no-nonsense people who enjoyed making decisions and liked to have control of their work. They were also a proud bunch who felt they had gotten their jobs in the first place because they were the best-qualified in their county (the last time the company posted eighteen jobs, more than four hundred people applied). The platform emphasized this in the first building block, which pointed out that the company hired the best and employees prove it every day with their talent, decisions, and hard work.

The second building block appealed to their sense of independence again, contrasting directly with how the company would operate if a union were involved and employees worked through union stewards. The third building block reminded employees that they have a stake in the union-organizing vote. The company continually invested in the plant and kept wages very competitive.

A Conversation Platform can frame an organization's overall strategic direction or focus in on one especially critical issue.

Finally, the fourth building block countered claims that employees would be better off as part of the union. It emphasized that employees are only as secure as the results they post, as indicated by the fact that the plant had not had any layoffs, while union sites did. In total, the company Conversation Platform was as depicted in Figure 7.2, with the cause, building blocks, and proof points.

Note that the platform speaks in the vernacular employees use in the plant—not corporate-speak. In fact, we wrote the building blocks using the actual words frontline supervisors used to describe what was special about their organization and why they didn't want a union involved. It didn't cover everything management talked about in their all-employee meetings, but it provided a way for supervisors to have conversations with employees about the union and hit the most important messages. They held those conversations informally in all kinds of locations, from the plant floor to the local tavern. It made them effective leadership communicators because the information was simple, and they could make it very relevant to employee situations. Consider this exchange, as related to us by one of the supervisors:

An employee came up to me and asked if he could leave early because his son had a soccer game. It was the championship game, and he really wanted to go.

I told him, no problem. But I also told him that if the union was here, I couldn't do that. I told him that we would have a lot of rules, and it wouldn't be like it is now, where we say how things are run. He'd have to go to the union steward, and I couldn't cover for him because I'm a supervisor and he's hourly. I went through each of the points, about how we're the best because we hire the best—something that would change with the union seniority system. And that all that stuff the union says about how a contract would protect everybody is a bunch of horse manure. [The supervisor didn't actually say "manure," but there are some limits to our recommendation to use the local vernacular.] I told him all that, and it made him think.

The supervisors made many employees think. They led the communication effort against a very tough union-organizing crowd. They were critical to the 3-to-1 margin win. They communicated as leaders should: in their own words, in a conversation that told a story, with concepts and information that were relevant to what employees cared about and that delivered results.

SUMMARY

Effective communication happens in the moment, when people are talking about the business and making decisions in their work areas. To enable leaders—from the CEO to a frontline supervisor—to communicate about strategy in the moment, they must be equipped with a message they can remember and deliver. That means the message has to be short—about five chunks of information. This five-chunk limit is driven by human short-term memory capacity.

The five chunks must be constructed to cover the key points of the Action Equation in the form of a very short story, not a separate laundry list of thoughts. The information must be articulated in the vernacular of day-to-day conversation, not corporate language. In fact, the chunks should be viewed as concepts employees can put into their own words, as opposed to lines of a script or slogans people are expected to repeat. We call this overall story the Conversation Platform.

The Conversation Platform is one of the most valuable and versatile tools leaders have at their disposal to improve leadership alignment and effective communication throughout the organization. It simplifies concepts to a point where they are easily remembered and articulated by top leaders, managers, supervisors, and employees alike. It enables all leaders to boil down the essence of where the organization is going and how it's going to get there (or to discuss complex, difficult issues facing employees and the business) in a short communication that could be delivered in an elevator ride or form the basis for a three-day conference on strategy and issues.

CHAPTER EIGHT

Align: Make Sure All Leaders Are On Strategy

—*ᴡᴡ*— "I do not rule Russia; ten thousand clerks do," Russia's Emperor Czar Nicholas said in 1825, frustrated over the lack of control he had over his country. He was a supreme autocrat, and he undoubtedly was referring to not only clerks stamping paperwork, but all of the people up and down his government bureaucracy. His inability to drive their behavior frustrated him, despite a pervasive network of secret police, censorship, and controls over all facets of public life.

It's very much like that in business (although even CEOs don't have quite that much power). Business leaders feel frustrated as strategy falters in the hands of vice presidents who pursue the wrong priorities, middle managers who sit on paperwork, and twenty-four-year-old customer service representatives who treat customers as no better than a nuisance. Not even the most hard-nosed leaders can fight the bureaucracy if it doesn't want to move.

Robert Nardelli learned this (at least we think he did) when he was CEO at Home Depot, although perhaps a few years too late. When he took the helm of the $46-billion company, he pushed hard to bring discipline to the organization. This included centralizing some functions, revamping inventory controls, and moving decision making away from local managers. He met stiff resistance, and much of the top executive team left during his first year. A year and a half into the effort, after trying to force-feed changes, Nardelli backtracked and began addressing the alignment issues he faced. "People never had time to grieve for the company Home Depot once was . . . and we didn't do a very good job of explaining the *why*," was how CFO Carol Time explained it.[1] The media and the market were unforgiving. Nardelli was widely criticized, and Home Depot's share price dropped from more than $40 when he assumed control in 2000 to just above $20 in 2003. When he finally started to get the organization aligned behind his strategy, performance improved. By then, however, it may have been too late. The Texas-based Investors for the Director Accountability Foundation targeted Nardelli as one of a handful of corporate executives who were paid too much, and he left the company in 2007 in a contentious battle with the board of directors over his pay. Perhaps alignment just wasn't in his blood, but it's clear it would have helped drive productive change in his company.

Effective leaders communicate and socialize a new direction at the outset of change, not years into it. Moreover, they involve seasoned leaders up and down the organization in designing and implementing tactical initiatives (such as changing new inventory control systems). This alignment begins with the top leadership of an organization, but then extends through management ranks. It has to be that way, or the clerks will bring change—and strategy execution—to a grinding halt.

DON'T BE FOOLED

The concept of *alignment* has become a popular—some say overused—business term. We use it here because it so accurately describes an essential step in leadership communication. For communication purposes, it involves agreement on a common message delivered to the organization. Its roots must be deeper than that, though. True alignment promotes the strategy that needs to be effectively communicated to employees. It is the synergy of direction and action up, down, and across an organization. When leadership is not truly aligned around strategy, leadership communication won't be either. As a result, strategy will falter.

> *True alignment of direction and action is an essential element of effective leadership communication.*

There are any number of methods now in use to drive leadership alignment—from multiyear working groups to weeklong team-building exercises to strategy boot camps. Depending on the alignment issue, any of these may be appropriate. If leaders are philosophically at odds about strategy or are being pulled apart by personal or political animosity, aggressive intervention like this makes sense.

If alignment issues stem from a misunderstanding of points of view or a lack of productive dialogue, or are more perceptual than real, communication can be the answer. Through communication you can surface issues, identify whether disagreements are real or perceived, and address them through conversation and dialogue. Alignment must be confirmed, though, not assumed. Just because managers nod "yes" in meetings doesn't mean they are aligned. Don't be fooled.

We worked, for example, with a vice president of manufacturing who needed to cut $150 million in costs across his manufacturing operations. He had seven facilities ranging in size from 600 to 4,500 employees. Through their individual plans, the seven plant managers reporting to him were able to identify about $90 million in cost reductions. That wasn't good enough. He had to try something new.

The vice president launched a new organizational operating strategy calling for increased collaboration across operations, integrating common resources and sharing accountability. In brief, the vice president wanted his plant management to operate not as seven distinct facilities but rather as a single organization. This was a dramatic change from the status quo.

The VP first presented the new approach with a forty-slide PowerPoint presentation that covered all the bases. He reviewed the cost-reduction goals and the rationale behind sharing and implementing best practices. "If our worst-performing departments can match the midpoint of our best-performing, we'll be able to meet our goals," he said. "Each plant performs similar work, and every plant has at least one best-in-company function. Let's learn from each other and get it right across the board." The managers nodded in agreement, and in the meeting talked about how they might work together. When the managers returned to their jobs, however, nothing changed. "They still don't talk to each other," the VP said. "And they certainly don't work together."

To remedy the situation, he went back to the drawing board. He condensed the strategy material into a simple, clear, document of about seven hundred words (not quite down to five hundred words, but still condensed). He then distributed the document to each of the plant managers and engaged us to follow up and interview each one about the strategy.

The intake sessions revealed that the plant managers understood the new direction, but there were a number of "why nots" rooted in the Behavior Chain that inhibited progress. "I see where he is going," one said. "But I'm not sure we can get there from here." The plant managers said the metrics governing their actions were both not uniform enough and too numerous for them to effectively evaluate best practices. Moreover, historically leadership had judged managers solely on the specific performance of their plant, and they had competed with each other for resources, recognition, and advancement. Now leadership was asking them to work together. They were concerned that this approach would put their careers at risk because either it would mask their individual successes or they would share in collective failures. Either way, it was a nonstarter. Moreover, there were issues outside their group that made collaboration difficult. Chief among these was conflicting direction given to them by senior executives from other functions, such as engineering, product management, and finance. Finally, they really didn't know how to work together as a team—they had never done it before. Putting teamwork into practice was much harder than just saying it in a document or talking about it in a meeting.

After reviewing these concerns, the VP brought his team together and worked through the issues in a structured conversation approach: consider-dialogue-solve (CDS, described later in this chapter). As a result, the plant managers began to collaborate, and they identified an additional $60 million in cost reductions within two months. Moreover, they communicated the need for increased collaboration to the managers in their organizations, and they began to communicate across plants. It started a new way of doing business that drove even greater cost savings and efficiencies.

START AT THE TOP AND WORK TO THE FRONT LINE

Using communication to drive action in support of strategy requires more than the top leader's commitment and effort. A critical step is ensuring that your leadership team—from the most senior executives to supervisors on the front line—are on the same page, with good understanding and support of the strategy. (After all, there's nothing more damaging to the success-

A thoughtful process behind strategy articulation can help ensure the clarity and alignment you need to be successful.

ful execution of a strategy than leaders providing different or even conflicting direction to employees.) In turn, that entire leadership group must communicate consistently to the entire organization. That takes alignment.

Informing the Action Equation (Chapters Three through Six), then distilling that information into a Conversation Platform (Chapter Seven) are the first steps to a communication-driven alignment process. The clear, concise description of strategy provided in the Action Equation makes it possible to identify differences of opinion among leaders. There is no complexity or ambiguity that can confuse issues or that they can hide behind.

The Conversation Platform helps distill the information even further and cements alignment around how leadership will talk about strategy with the organization. We've found it effective to use both tools to engage leadership teams in strategy discussions.

Once a leader has completed his or her homework by informing the Action Equation and creating a first-draft Conversation Platform, it's time to ensure that the top leadership team is on the same page. To do this, we suggest engaging a third party to conduct one-on-one interviews with each member of the top leadership team—the core leadership group. Using an intermediary to conduct this intake increases the chance that disagreements or misunderstandings will surface. This facilitator/interviewer can be a staff member people trust or someone from outside your organization. Ideally, this person can facilitate the entire process, from information gathering to eventual alignment.

In these intake meetings, the facilitator can confirm understanding and agreement on the Action Equation and Conversation Platform and surface any concerns or issues of the individual executives. The facilitator can also ask questions to identify any "why nots" that stand in the way of alignment. These include issues around commitment, trust, philosophical disagreements, groupthink, and conflicting direction from various leaders and others. These are the kinds of issues that leaders don't often raise with each other, or among employees, but can in the end derail strategy execution. From these discussions, the facilitator can create a Situation Snapshot designed to outline the issues and get them on the table for discussion. (We include suggested questions for intake meetings and for creating a Situation Snapshot in the "How to" Resource Guide, Chapter Twelve.)

With the Situation Snapshot and Conversation Platform in hand, a leader is ready to talk about them with his or her team and to drive alignment. For some teams, this kind of discussion is very natural. People are open to sharing ideas, exchanging perspectives, and identifying alternative solutions. For many others, that kind of open dialogue can be challenging, but not insurmountable, given the right tools and approach.

PROMOTE OPEN DISCUSSION AT MULTIPLE LEVELS

Management styles in many organizations, particularly those with a Command communication profile, do not encourage conversation and real dialogue among teams or individuals. One of the most prevalent counterproductive practices in team discussion is to skip or gloss over dialogue that considers the problem, moving quickly to discussion around solutions. Because of this, the depth and complexity of problems are often misunderstood and important considerations are ignored. To truly work through strategy issues as a team, it takes dialogue in which people share ideas, listen to each other, and discuss disagreements. The consider-dialogue-solve (CDS) framework, which we developed to improve alignment and communication at the team level, helps promote this kind of discussion.

The intention of the CDS framework is to provide a team with an approach and tools to ensure that they can have a rich exchange of perspective and ideas and come to a place of true alignment, not just surface agreement. The CDS framework has three steps. In the first (consider), team members share topic information well before the meeting is held to discuss it. This gives people time to consider the information, talk to others in their work area

Use a deliberate process before and during meetings to promote dialogue.

about their perspectives, and prepare for the discussion that is to take place. In the second step (dialogue), which takes place at the meeting, those attending discuss as a group the topic information and issues without moving right into identifying solutions. This promotes a deeper understanding of the information, issues, and the causes behind problems. It also enables people to see and understand conflicting perspectives and points of view. When teams jump too quickly to problem solving, this kind of deep understanding is lost. In the final step (solve), all discuss solutions and select those that the group believes will be most effective.

A word of caution: with seriously dysfunctional teams, the CDS framework will be only marginally effective. If senior leaders are chronic command-and-control managers, or if the team faces deep issues around trust, it's very difficult to promote dialogue. Such challenges must be addressed separately, usually through one-on-one coaching with a professional or through intense team-building work. CDS is, however, an effective tool for most teams, especially when implemented by a seasoned facilitator.

Once the senior team is aligned around the Conversation Platform, it's time to take it all to the field. As you move deeper into the organization, it becomes less practical to conduct facilitated intake. The number of managers and time constraints make that level of interaction difficult. It's still important to test your messaging with the larger organization, however. Just as a consumer products company wouldn't ask every consumer what they thought of a new product design, they wouldn't introduce one without testing it with a reasonable cross section of the population. We recommend the same approach with the messages you intend to take to your larger organization, using the "red face" test.

The "red face" test determines whether managers can and will communicate leadership's message to the organization, or whether they will get "red-faced" with embarrassment or anger over its content. This is a critical step in communicating through the People Channel. First, it reveals whether the senior team's perception of reality is different from that of employees closer to the front line. Second, the "red face" test reveals whether the Conversation Platform expresses strategy in terms and language employees will understand and support. Third, by involving a small group of key managers and supervisors in the process, top leaders begin to build support for strategy among the leaders deeper in the organization.

The basis of the "red face" test is the Conversation Platform. A facilitator simply shows the platform to managers and supervisors and asks them a series of questions. (A review of how to conduct the "red face" test is included in Chapter Twelve.) We recently worked with an insurance company, for example, that was shifting its strategy to ensure that it could deliver on not only the insurance but also the financial planning needs of its clients. This shift in strategy required significant changes in the operation of the business as well as in the behaviors of its employees and agents. Before leaders took the new strategy directly to employees and agents, they conducted the "red face" test in small discussion groups and through one-on-one conversations. As a result, leaders learned first that they needed to clarify the meaning behind some of the key elements of the strategy. For example, their "cause" or core message spoke to the leadership's focus on becoming the "best" in their industry. Although the meaning and measurement of the "best" was clear at the executive level, employees needed more context. One employee said, "Saying we want to be 'the best' is admirable, but I want a picture in my mind of what it looks like." Another employee asked, "How do we know when we are the best?" These were legitimate questions, and hearing this feedback from employees helped leadership to reconsider how they spoke about "the best" and how they would measure it.

The feedback wasn't centered just on language. The groups also surfaced employee and management concerns about the organization's ability to execute the strategy. For example, managers recognized how much the organization already asked of its agents, and they were concerned that some agents would not be able to handle the added workload the strategy required. Actually, the leadership team had recognized these issues long before and had already put some project teams in place to address the potential overload issue, but managers and employees weren't yet aware of those efforts. Coming out of these discussion groups, leadership committed to increase the visibility of programs designed specifically to ensure that agents had the resources and skills to be able to succeed under this new strategy.

Test your messaging in the field before rolling it out. This will save time and resources in the long run.

In another organization, leaders built a Conversation Platform that included five key metrics. When they conducted the "red face" test with frontline supervisors, the local leaders balked. Employees, they said, were very disheartened by recent failures, so it would be difficult to motivate them to embrace the overall strategy until they had seen some short-term success. The supervisors thought that if they could focus on just two metrics and show progress on them, it would do a lot to improve the employee mindset and ultimately would help the supervisors mobilize employees to support the strategy with energy and commitment. With this feedback, leadership established just two immediate goals; the other goals they referred to as longer-term objectives. In a short time, employees saw progress on those metrics and became more confident in their ability to be successful. As time passed, leadership added the other metrics to the short-term mix and continued to build momentum and make progress.

INCLUDE INFORMAL LEADERS IN THE PEOPLE CHANNEL

Aligning your leadership team—from senior executives to frontline supervisors—around your Conversation Platform is a critical step in leadership communication. Alignment goes beyond the formal structure of the organization, however. If you limit those included in this alignment process to just those leaders who are in the boxes

The informal leader network is a valuable resource that should be tapped into and supported.

on the organization chart, you're potentially missing a large and very powerful group that you need to have on your side to be successful. We refer to this important group as *informal leaders*.

There are leaders as depicted in the organization chart, and there are leaders who have people who follow them. These two are not always the same. The latter group is a powerful component of the People Channel. They are the individuals others turn to informally for information, perspective, and even direction, whether they report to that person or not. For example, an employee might hear news or direction from their direct supervisor but go to somebody else in the organization to discuss it and get confirmation and perspective.

Informal leaders can be part of the formal leadership group—executives, managers, supervisors, and the like. They also very well may reside outside that structure, ranging from a union steward to the receptionist who always seems to have the inside scoop.

Informal leaders often have an even more influential voice in an organization than many formal leaders do. They can act as "third-party endorsers" of a strategy or an initiative—and their influence is two-way. They not only communicate to employees but also are a great source of feedback and buzz from the organization. In many organizations, the informal leaders make or break a communication effort. It may be hard to believe that the receptionist could have more sway in shaping opinions than an executive, but it's true. This is particularly true in organizations whose executives don't get out of their offices much. (This is true in politics as well—most presidential candidates would love to have the local bartender or hairdresser on their side.) Therefore, it is critically important to include your informal leaders in the alignment process. Their help, over time, will do a lot to drive strategy and get results. The "How to" Resource Guide (Chapter Twelve) contains specific guidance on how to identify and engage informal leaders.

SUMMARY

Top leaders need help communicating with their organizations—they can't do it alone. Therefore, a leader must align his or her leadership group behind strategy and communication, starting with top leadership and then extending the alignment all the way down to frontline supervisors. Without this kind of alignment, employees head in different directions, work at cross-purposes, and derail strategy execution.

The first step in aligning leadership behind strategy and communications is to begin with the senior leadership team. We recommend enlisting the help of a seasoned, trusted facilitator to interview each member of the leadership team, using the Action Equation as a basis for intake. These intake sessions identify differences in understanding, perception, philosophy, and other factors that may divide the leadership team. They also will uncover deeper motivational issues around trust and commitment that can inhibit collaboration. The output from these meetings helps drive productive discussion among the top leaders to resolve their issues and get on the same page.

Once top leadership is aligned, we recommend taking messages (in the form of the Conversation Platform) to the field and testing them with line managers and supervisors. This determines whether line managers will support the strategy and how leaders want to communicate it. Just as a good marketing company wouldn't introduce a major new product without testing it with customers, leaders shouldn't take important messages to the organization without first ensuring that they will work. In working to align the organization behind the strategy, don't miss one of the most important constituencies—the informal leaders to whom those individuals turn for information and perspective. They may or may not be found in the leadership boxes on the organizational chart, but their influence in the organization is undeniable.

CHAPTER NINE

Equip: Give Leaders the Tools They Need to Communicate On Strategy

We recently attended a management meeting at a large technology company where the CEO outlined the strategies that were designed to take the company "to the next level." After he walked through the content of the strategies with a PowerPoint presentation and video, the final slide directed the leadership group to communicate the strategy to their employees. It provided a few tips on communication—"techniques you already know," according to the CEO. Also, he said the communications department would provide managers with a PowerPoint presentation and video package to adapt for their local groups. The CEO said it was essential to reach every employee with the presentation. The managers nodded in agreement, and they fully intended to deliver on that direction.

It was like sending Paris Hilton to milk the cows on the television show *The Simple Life*. Give her a pail. She knows where the parts are and how it's supposed to work, so she should do it. If you haven't seen Paris milk a cow, it's worth a few laughs. But sending a group of managers to communicate critical strategies with a PowerPoint presentation and video isn't a laughing matter—it's a problem waiting to happen. Just as Paris would need some help to fill the pail, managers need to be trained and equipped to communicate strategy. Just because they have a presentation and can get up in front of a group and talk doesn't mean they are prepared to communicate on strategy—especially if that strategy represents a change in direction, has met resistance from the organization, or needs to be executed in times of stress or uncertainty. They need training and support.

You say somebody else in your organization is responsible for training? Before you skip to the next chapter, stop. We're not talking about skills training on how to give a presentation or manage a meeting. We're talking about training on the specific strategy your company is engaged in executing. As such, the training needed is as much about explaining strategy as about providing managers with a way to communicate to others. That's a leadership responsibility, and not something to be delegated in full to the training or communication departments. At the same time, it can be very helpful to engage training and communication people in developing the approach for your company, and to get their assistance in delivering the training, particularly if it involves large groups. Use them to build a robust program to fulfill the requirements outlined in the following sections. They can use what we provide as a starting point to build a tailored On Strategy communication approach to training and ongoing support of the People Channel. But make it your responsibility to lead this effort, and model that commitment for the rest of the managers and supervisors in the organization.

TRAIN LEADERS AS IF STRATEGY DEPENDED ON IT

Companies train managers in every important facet of business except strategy communication. Somehow, managers are supposed to just know how to communicate strategy. That's a mistake. Most people have certain abilities to communicate—just as a sales person has a baseline ability to sell, no matter what the product is. But a company wouldn't ask the sales force to sell a product without training them in how the product works. The same goes for strategy. On Strategy communication requires that managers understand strategy and how to communicate it.

On Strategy training, as we outline it, will take about two to three hours at the outset, with coaching and support following the initial session. It's important to consider who leads the training. Ideally, a senior leader should deliver the training, because the content is strategy, not skills. As such, On Strategy training is very much like a presentation and discussion about strategy—and who better to lead such a discussion than the executives who have developed the strategy? Executive involvement also demonstrates that On Strategy communication is a high priority for the company. With that in mind, it's reasonable that a CEO would lead the training (which might better be called a briefing) for the organization's senior executives, then those executives would lead it for the next level, and so on through each level of the organization. This approach not only delivers strategy to each level of the organization but also enables managers to tailor the information to their work area. Moreover, this approach deepens manager knowledge of strategy as they prepare and present it to their people. It's helpful to have assistance while conducting the training, especially if the groups are large. If you decide to use trainers as the primary deliverers of the training, at the very least you should ask a senior business leader to kick off the session, welcome participants, and let them know why this session is so important. The leader can then speak about the People Channel and the critical role that every leader down through frontline supervisors will play in making it successful. The training should cover six areas, as follows.

Set Expectations. At the outset, set expectations about manager and supervisor responsibilities for communication. Outline the important connection between communication and results and the critical role that managers and supervisors play in the communication process. It's important to explain that effective communication will also help the managers get their jobs done, because the communi-

> *Training on strategy is a leadership responsibility best delivered by leaders, assisted by staff.*

cation is about strategy execution and how it relates to their job and responsibilities, not abstract corporate issues. Cover the methods by which executive leadership will measure and track manager performance in communication (this concrete performance management is important—it puts action to the words). This is an ideal time for a senior leader to provide examples of his or her commitment to communication; how it has helped achieve results and get the job done. The leader can also take this opportunity to make a commitment to the leadership group that the senior team will keep them in the loop, wants to hear from them as issues and challenges are raised, and appreciates their time and effort.

Introduce the Conversation Platform. Review the concept of the Conversation Platform and how it will be used to frame leadership's strategic message. This review is essential for first-time users of the Conversation Platform. Most people aren't familiar with brevity in strategy communication, especially as structured in a platform. They need to be confident that the process works before they try to use it. The concept review portion of the training answers the following questions:

- What is a Conversation Platform?
- Why are we using a Conversation Platform?
- How should we use it?
- How shouldn't we use it?
- How will it help me as a manager?

Review Specific Content. The content-review portion of the training introduces managers to the specific content of the platform—it trains managers in strategy itself. Participants must understand that feedback is welcome, but that strategy is not up for debate during the training. The purpose of the training is communication, not strategy development.

It's most effective to walk through the platform chunk by chunk, starting with the core message or "cause," then sharing each of the four building blocks. Delve deeply into each of the four building blocks to walk through the specific actions, or proof points, the organization is taking to implement each strategy. Use interactive exercises to build involvement and ensure understanding. For example, ask the managers to identify programs and initiatives in which they are involved, and how those fit into the building blocks of the Conversation Platform. Discuss those that don't seem to fit, then work to resolve them. If the local managers are, in fact, involved with work that is not on strategy, discuss actions the managers might take to address that issue. (If staff people are

Effective training grounds leaders on the strategy and how to talk about it with employees every day.

delivering the training, coach the managers on dealing with these issues, or involve more senior managers in the discussion as well.) Also, provide a list of potential employee questions about the strategies that make up the Conversation Platform. Then ask participants to identify which part of the Conversation Platform would help to answer each of the employee questions. You can break the group into several smaller groups to discuss the platform and answer the questions, then share their findings with the larger group.

It's also important to review in detail the "whys" and "why nots" in the platform, whether they are implicit or explicit. As we've pointed out before, it's critical to combine the rational and intrinsic motivations of employees in communication on an ongoing basis. At every opportunity, leaders must address each area of the Action Equation: Know + Feel = Do.

Use the Platform. The fourth element of the training gives leaders an opportunity to practice using the platform in conversations with employees or colleagues. To do this, we recommend a role-play session, with participants taking turns acting as employee and manager. Use the same list of potential employee questions as used in the content review, but also include some surprises. This exercise is especially important because the People Channel works most effectively when managers communicate through conversations. Managers must be comfortable delivering strategic messages through conversation, and this role-play exercise helps achieve that.

It's also important to remind participants at this point that they should not recite the platform verbatim, but put the concepts in their own words. The platform provides the essence of the message, but to avoid sounding like corporate propaganda, it must be presented in the actual words of the individual manager. Share examples of how other managers deliver the platform and role-play so the managers in the current training can frame how they will use the platform and articulate the messaging. Because the platform is also used to frame more formal communication—such as presentations, speeches, and business reports—the training should cover how the platform should influence those as well. An effective way to do this is to share examples, such as a speech or newsletter article, in "before" and "after" forms: examples that do not consider the platform, each followed by a version that employs the platform as a filter and content tool. In the manager training sessions this should be reviewed conceptually, but you should also consider training sessions designed specifically for communicators across the organization. Those responsible for internal and external communication (HR, Marketing, Training, Recruiting, Communications) need to have an even deeper understanding of how to use the Conversation Platform as a filter in formal communication.

Process Review. Once the managers have a good grasp of the Conversation Platform and how to use it, the next element of the training is to outline the process and tools that are in place to support leaders on an ongoing basis. Make it clear that, concerning strategy, the leadership of the organization is the primary communication channel in the company. The other channels, such as newsletters and large meetings, are there to support them in communicating to employees, not to replace them. Assuming changes are under way to enhance the organization's overall communication process (as described in Chapter Ten), stress that there is a concerted effort under way to strengthen the strategic focus and design of the current employee-directed channels (newsletter, intranet, and so on) and share some of the progress of those projects as well. Explain, also, that the company and its leadership will provide ongoing support to managers in their communication efforts. Discuss in some detail the specific communication channel established to keep managers informed (which we'll address shortly) and how that channel will be used. Show how all the pieces fit together into a cohesive process to support the leadership group.

Ask for Feedback. Ask the managers to give their feedback on the overall process and how they believe it could be improved. Take suggestions seriously and make changes. Also, be sure to report back to the managers on what happened to their suggestions. This can be done through a separate memo, or through the manager-direct communication channel outlined shortly.

The frequency with which you conduct this type of training depends on a variety of factors. It's important to conduct a comprehensive training of your entire leadership group (supervisors up through senior leadership) with the initial launch of your Conversation Platform. After that, train new members to the leadership group as soon as possible—ideally as part of the onboarding process. This provides a solid introduction to strategy, eliminates avoidable mistakes and confusion that new managers may make regarding strategy execution, and equips new leaders to join and support ongoing strategy communication.

When top leadership changes the Conversation Platform, the People Channel doesn't necessarily require an entirely new training effort. Communicate changes to the leaders, and give them the opportunity to ask questions and seek clarification. If, for example, you have an upcoming major event (such as labor negotiations, possible mergers, going public), you may choose to build a separate but complementary message platform to ensure that leaders have the depth of information and context they need on that particular subject to have effective conversations with employees. In those cases, we recommend reviewing the new platform with managers so they understand the content, and working through role-play situations so they are comfortable delivering it.

SUPPORT LOCAL LEADERS AND THE PEOPLE CHANNEL

The People Channel—the leaders up and down the organization— must be in the loop and one step ahead of the general employee population. These people will share information and provide a local interpretation and perspective on strategy, so they must fully understand strategy, be aware of communication events, and be prepared to answer questions. Training leaders on the strategy and how to communicate with employees about it is the first step in preparing the leadership team. The next step is to set up a system to ensure that leaders are getting the information and insight they need to be a reliable channel in the eyes and experiences of employees. No manager or supervisor likes to look poorly informed or ignorant in front of the employees they supervise. If they do, they tend to just blame it on poor leadership, turning the problem into a complaint: "Nobody tells me anything." Or "I don't get it—they don't know what they are doing."

Keep Leaders Updated

Keeping the People Channel informed is relatively simple and inexpensive, and there are many opportunities to do so. If you commit to the mindset that leaders need to know and understand information before the greater population does, then some small adjustments to current communication practices may fit the bill. For example, when an executive visits a location to meet with employees, make sure he or she meets with managers and supervisors first. As part of the communication, provide those managers and supervisors with background material that will be helpful in communicating to their employees. The information presented to that group can be more expansive and deeper than that presented to the larger employee group. In addition, this type of meeting provides an opportunity to answer questions, clarify issues, and even role-play difficult questions employees may be asking.

Another good opportunity for People Channel learning arises when a public company holds conference calls about results with analysts. Follow the analyst call with a leaders-only conference call to address the issues raised by analysts and answer questions. This provides even greater context for strategy and the pressure that affects the executive team. Sometimes analyst calls can get quite heated; hearing them firsthand and then discussing them can help build a sense of urgency among the leaders. Moreover, this technique helps ensure that the leadership team is prepared to explain the results to employees in the context of the bigger picture and to more confidently answer employee questions.

A reliable way to keep the People Channel informed is to create a simple, dedicated communication piece directed to the leaders who form the channel. One company, for example, ensures the effectiveness of their People Channel with a management-only, one-page electronic brief distributed monthly to the entire management team. The newsletter includes a heads-up of upcoming actions, news that illustrates how the company is executing its strategy, recaps of recent events, and Q&A to address current rumors or buzz in the organization. The publication also gives managers and supervisors advance notice of the content of the next employee newsletter so they can be prepared to direct employees to the articles and answer potential questions. In addition to the leaders-only monthly brief, the company also produces an immediate-notification vehicle for them. This brief addresses specific issues or news that can't wait for the monthly manager newsletter. For example, rumors were circulating at one company about a controversial article in the *Wall Street Journal* related to the business, and this immediate response vehicle provided perspective on the article and answered employee questions the same day the article appeared.

Various other channels can be effective in keeping managers and supervisors in the loop and serving as strong communicators, so keep them in mind not only for their specific local purpose but also for On Strategy communication. These channels include the following:

- *Operating meetings.* Functions and departments usually have periodic meetings among managers and supervisors to talk about production goals, problems, and so on. They don't last long and are very focused. Use them to update managers and supervisors on what they need to know to support leadership communication.

- *Reporting documents.* Various functions, particularly finance and human resources, continually issue reports. Use them not only to convey the specific information they're designed to deliver, but also to organize them strategically and include relevant On Strategy information and perspective.

- *Information package(s) with write-ups, visuals, and the like for each manager and supervisor.* Managers and supervisors will have time to read an information kit if it's brief and engaging. As needed, distribute the information in segments so it's easy to digest.

- *Intranet site.* Some companies create a password-protected intranet site for managers and supervisors. The site can be a good way to make announcements, provide in-depth background, and offer consistent answers for leadership to use with common employee questions.

- *Conference calls.* Before making announcements to the general employee population, have managers and supervisors participate in a conference call in which you can give them the information they need and answer questions.

- *Telephone hotline.* Some managers and supervisors don't have ready access to computers, but they can call in. Set up a hotline for them so they can stay in the loop.

For some topics—those more complex or controversial—it's important not only to share the information in advance with the leadership group, but also to give them an opportunity to digest the information and get answers to the questions they and their employees will have. Organizations often try to address this by providing leaders with a Q&A document. That approach can be valuable, but it assumes those who prepare the Q&A can anticipate all the questions leaders and employees may have—which is not always the case. It's also very difficult to provide nuance or deeper perspective around issues through a document. It can get very lengthy and therefore hard to digest. Moreover, those documents often are vetted through any number of filters, such as legal, HR, finance, and others. They can easily become diluted, or very confusing—the kind of babble that On Strategy communication must avoid. Therefore, an opportunity for a live conversation among the leadership group, supported by written documentation like a Q&A, is the best way to ensure that leaders are truly prepared to talk with employees about the specifics of the topic at hand.

It's critical to have an effective system in place to ensure that leaders are always informed before the larger employee population is.

The People Channel thrives on a solid system of continuous information flow between senior leaders and the rest of the leadership team. Each organization is different, and each should select tools and channels that work within the culture, structure, geography, and other factors that affect information flow. However, there are some basic principles every organization should follow.

It's usually obvious that major announcements and changes need to be communicated through the People Channel, but there's more to it than that. Ideally, any topic of conversation—the events, communication, changes, or other triggers that generate conversations among employees—should be addressed through the People Channel. Moreover, any event, communication, change, or other situation that leadership wants employees to talk about is appropriate to drive through the People Channel. These include the following:

- Visible and measurable progress (or shortfalls) against strategy and goals
- Any decisions that would alter or shift the focus of the organization
- Personnel changes—hiring or firing of any significance in the organization
- Major issues related to your customers, products, or both

• Industry news and events that are relevant to your business

• Any public announcements

• Rumors that are circulating

If there is any question whether information is relevant or not, get in touch with some of the informal leadership of the organization and test it. The People Channel certainly shouldn't be filled with anything that resembles babble, but it works best when managers and supervisors are fully informed of issues employees will be talking about in their conversations.

Promote an Ongoing Leadership Conversation

People communicate through conversations. That goes for leaders as well as all employees, so it is important to promote ongoing conversation at the leadership level. Provide opportunities for your leadership group to get together as a team. In today's business environment, there is a constant push to do more with less and faster. In that mode, far too many organizations have scaled back dramatically on the time they allow leaders to spend doing anything that doesn't have an immediate impact on the bottom line. This is unfortunate and detrimental to longer-term results. As any good leader knows, taking a little time to be thoughtful, share ideas, and consider next steps can pay off greatly in the short and long term. That's why we strongly encourage clients to invest the time it takes to bring leaders together periodically to share progress, talk about challenges, and, most important, to get to know each other. Those experiences are irreplaceable in building a truly cohesive and effective leadership team that is capable of taking on the hardest of challenges. The depth of understanding and feeling of engagement that leaders take away from effective gatherings can have a significant impact on the success of the People Channel.

RECOGNIZE AND STRENGTHEN THE WEAK LINKS

Most people can have a productive conversation. There are those, however, who can't. That's an important consideration. Leadership style has a strong impact on the success or failure of the People Channel. Leaders set the ground rules for conversation, whether they intend to or not. As they do, they either promote conversation or turn people into bystanders. For example, some leaders manage discussions with employees in a "tell and respond" style in which the leader barks out questions and expects answers. Intimidated employees offer the safest answers to questions, often leaving out important details. In another style, "solutions only," leaders cut short the conversations associated with problem identification and immediately move to problem solving in an effort to be more productive. This style doesn't allow people to explore the complexity, nuance, or depth of problems, and it often results in superficial solutions. Likewise, leaders who intimidate and create an environment based on fear, or who embarrass employees who bring forward negative information, will stifle On Strategy communication.

Leadership's views on "attitude" also play a role in either promoting or stifling conversation. For example, one organization we worked with was intent on promoting a "positive attitude," defined by an employee's expressed optimism about whether problems would be solved, regardless of the challenges faced. Consequently, employees who challenged the effectiveness of solutions or pointed out additional problems appeared to leadership to not have a "positive attitude." This stifled On Strategy communication and resulted in the implementation of half-baked solutions and a refusal to acknowledge indications of trouble.

Culture and style can have a direct impact on the ability of employees and leaders to have real conversations about strategy.

Another situation along the same lines developed when leadership at a company continually told employees, "When you come to me with a problem, bring a solution along as well." This was a legitimate attempt to ensure that employees owned the problems they identified rather than pushing them off on leaders; however, as a result, leaders and employees seldom had productive conversations about problems, and if they did, those discussions were delayed. Employees feared raising a problem before they had a solution, and sometimes solutions came somewhat late in decision-making cycles.

Training can make a difference for leaders who have difficulty communicating. Again, the training we recommend most is not the typical communication skills training. There's nothing wrong with that, but the most important training for the People Channel involves interpersonal skills. These skills include the ability to listen, to pay attention despite distractions and pressure, and to empathize

Train leaders on interpersonal skills, and if a manager doesn't have what it takes, pair him or her with somebody who does.

with people. A number of organizations provide excellent training and coaching in this area. Look for a partner in this area that has flexibility in how it delivers the training. Senior leaders need coaching more than training, so an organization that offers professional leadership coaching is very valuable. Building interpersonal skills on large teams can also be very important. We were involved with one company that trained as many as a thousand employees at a time in daylong sessions. It was very powerful.

The interpersonal skills training should focus on the ability to

- Establish rapport with superiors, subordinates, and peers
- Listen without resistance, while also evaluating hard data to get answers to problems
- Recognize when employees are evading issues and draw out information from them
- Overcome issues that individuals have about communicating, ranging from fear of reprisal to extreme introversion
- Create an environment in which productive discussion can flourish

COMPLEMENTARY LEADER ASSIGNMENTS

Sometimes, however, people just don't have what it takes, at least without intensive interpersonal training and intervention. In those cases, they need a different kind of support. For example, we worked with a cross-functional team charged with a critical manufacturing realignment. According to the company's president, "The success of the initiative would make or break us for the next three years." He asked us to observe the team responsible for execution, because he considered communication critical to success.

We met with the team leader, Tom, and watched him communicate with the twenty-two people on his team. He was very intelligent, with great intensity and dedication. He was also very diligent concerning communication. Each team member kept detailed project management logs, and they all met once every two weeks for a day to review the state of the realignment. They spent a lot of time on trying to communicate, but it was a waste of time. Here's how the meeting looked:

Tom opened the meeting and passed out a detailed agenda based on the activity logs each of the managers kept up to date. There were usually about forty active job streams going on at any given time. The agenda called for going through each one, and it was tight. There was no room for anything else. He would always point out, "There is a lot to cover here, so we don't have time to waste. We must keep to the schedule." And keep to it they did. No matter what came up, he was determined to cover every topic, even if it meant cutting off discussion about a critical situation. Of the twenty-two people on the team besides Tom, only a handful talked more than once or twice during the eight-hour meetings. Even when critical problems came up, most people were silent. Tom made no effort to bring those people into the discussion.

When the meeting concluded, Tom asked us what we thought about the communication approach. We did our best to be supportive, but explained that it was not very effective. The team seldom, if ever, discussed difficult issues. The agenda hog-tied them. People didn't have enough time to sort through the clutter or get comfortable talking about possible failure. Moreover, many people didn't contribute during the meeting. They appeared intimidated by the process, and we doubted they would raise problems that the team needed to address. We made four suggestions:

1. Create a summary of the action logs to update people on progress and provide that to people before the meeting.

2. Focus the meetings on problems the team needs to address, not every single action item.

3. Let the group self-select the issues they need to talk about, and give them time to work through the agenda in a less structured way. There must be free time for discussion.

4. Work to build participation by people who didn't appear engaged, either during the meeting or before and after.

Tom rejected each of our suggestions. He said, "Every work stream is critical, and I don't want to miss problems by not talking about each one. We're giving people every opportunity to communicate. If they don't step up to the plate, it's not my problem." In the end, it would be his problem when the realignment failed.

We brought this up to the company president, as he requested, and he was not surprised by Tom's attitude. "Tom is a command and control guy," he said. "He would never think to actually seek out information in any form but a command. As far as working through things with less structure, he'd rather lay on a bed of nails than let loose of any control. But he's great at organizing things. He knows what all the parts need to do to make the realignment successful. We can't lose that."

We suggested that Tom receive structured interpersonal skills training, but in the meantime have a coleader on the team (who was strong in this area) responsible for communication. That way, the group would benefit from Tom's organizational skills, but also work better as a team.

It was a sound solution. Some people just aren't equipped to be good communicators, at least right now. Complement them with other leaders with stronger communication skills, especially when they are in charge of teams.

SUMMARY

Businesses train top leaders, managers, and supervisors in many things, but seldom train them about strategy and how to communicate it. We strongly recommend training with this purpose. This isn't skill training, but content training, and as such should be a prerequisite of any leader's participation in the management of the business. Moreover, because it's content training—it's about strategy—leaders should be active in delivering the training.

We recommend developing a training approach organized around the Conversation Platform and Action Equation, focusing on the core message or "cause," the building blocks, and the proof points. This helps create a common understanding and delivery method for strategy communication (it also helps deepen the understanding managers and supervisors have of strategy). With the platform as a foundation, we suggest the training be used to:

- Develop a solid understanding of strategy among managers and supervisors
- Ground leaders in what the Conversation Platform is and how it's used
- Build understanding of the communication processes the organization will use to communicate strategy and support managers
- Get feedback

In addition to training, we suggest providing ongoing communication support tailored specifically to managers and supervisors. This includes a communication process or vehicle to keep them updated on strategy so they know news before the rest of the organization and therefore can help communicate and provide perspective. This should include the opportunity to ask questions. Concerning skills training, we recommend a focus on interpersonal rather than communication techniques. Improving in that area will provide the most benefit, because On Strategy communication asks people to talk to each other as opposed to making presentations and speeches (it also requires listening, which is a rare capability among many managers).

Finally, we recognize that some managers (a smaller number than you might think) will not become effective enough in communication to deliver On Strategy messages—at least in time to have an immediate impact on performance. In those cases, we recommend pairing those managers with others who are effective communicators to provide better direction and motivation to the employees and teams they lead. That way the leaders serve immediate communication needs relative to performance, help the deficient leader learn how to communicate better, and show the rest of the organization that communication is a critical leadership capability.

CHAPTER TEN

Drive and Support: Orchestrate and Sustain On Strategy Conversation

—⁓— "I want to get on top of the building and shout: Let's get going! I want to put up a giant thermometer like the ones for blood drives to show where we are and how far we have to go. I want to get some action."

That's what a frustrated executive told us as he vented about his organization. He had taken over his organization a year earlier, and he was not getting the cooperation or intensity he needed for the company to be successful. He intuitively knew part of the problem was communication. He was right on every count.

A leader must drive communication. It doesn't just happen. After you finish the Action Equation, build the Conversation Platform, align and equip your leadership team, and establish the People Channel, you still have to kick-start the communication and keep it going on a continuous basis. The challenge is to establish a disciplined system of process and vehicles that ensures that leadership shares the right information with employees, and that the People Channel is ready to maximize the opportunity through conversation. Moreover, as you do this, continue to ensure that these vehicles support the People Channel; they do not replace it. Ultimately, the managers and supervisors in the organization deliver strategy messages, not the company newsletter or Intranet. These are support tools, not the primary means of delivery.

That said, we offer three recommendations to govern communication vehicles that support the People Channel. First, use those vehicles to create a continuous "drumbeat" of communication, starting with the vehicles you already have and making them more effective. Second, when you need to turn up the communication volume, do so with targeted, short-term "campaigns." Finally, look to the communications department or outside resources for help. By following these three recommendations, leaders find they can build a communication capability in their organization without the need to climb to the top of the building and shout (or to spend excessive time and money).

CREATE A DRUMBEAT

Ongoing On Strategy communication creates a continuous drumbeat of information, insight, and perspective about strategy, directed to stakeholders who are critical to strategy execution. Employees should see the messages of the Conversation Platform everywhere they look, and leadership should use every opportunity to get the messages in front of them.

Maximize All the Vehicles Available

Most companies already have plenty of communication vehicles in place to support On Strategy communication. So before you launch a new vehicle, shape up those you have already. For our purposes, we break vehicles down into "traditional" and "operating" vehicles. The traditional vehicles are those often mentioned when people talk about communication: newsletters, town hall meetings, the intranet site, and the like. The operating vehicles are those that are integral to the day-to-day running of the business: regular reporting documents, operating review meetings, functional and departmental meetings, and the other ways in which managers communicate in the course of doing their jobs. Operating and traditional vehicles alike can provide powerful opportunities to communicate on strategy, but it takes process and discipline.

Babble clutters much of the message stream produced by communication vehicles in many companies, and it gets in the way.

We conducted an audit of one major company's traditional communication vehicles and measured the babble in pounds—literally. We asked a representative group of managers to keep three boxes in their work area. One box, labeled Valuable, was for communication they received that helped them to do their job. Another box—labeled Helpful—was for information that was nice to have. And the box labeled Rather Not Get was for information that was a waste of time. After a month, we checked the boxes and measured the material in the Valuable and Helpful boxes in ounces. We had to triple the size of the Rather Not Get box to continue the audit, as the babble overflowed onto the floor.

You might want to blame the communication department for this, and often they are part of the problem. But the babble goes well beyond their work to include the communication produced by functions across the organization—from Human Resources to IT to the people who run the cafeteria. In fact, one senior communication professional made this point at a company conference by collecting all of the newsletters, booklets, binders, videos, and other communication he received from across the company, which his department didn't produce. He put them in a wheelbarrow and dumped them out in front of the audience—and had to make two trips. He implored his fellow managers to stop creating new forms of communication, and to work with him to stop the babble.

Technology is part of the problem. The information age could easily be renamed the age of information overload. First there was just the memo, and only as many copies as a typewriter with carbon paper could make. Then came the mimeograph, and the copier, and the unlimited ability to duplicate messages on paper. Desktop publishing followed, with a proliferation of flyers, newsletters, and three-ring binders. Now, with the Internet and email, the babble is reaching epic proportions. It's time to put an end to all this by focusing communication where it should be—on strategy.

Traditional communication vehicles are an important part of the People Channel. They inform conversation by disseminating information and acting as a reliable resource for employees. They also can generate strategy conversations between the People Channel and employees, and among employees. To deliver these benefits, however, the traditional vehicles must deliver on three levels. First, content must be on strategy. Second, the communication must be compelling enough to generate interest and conversation. Third, communication about strategy must be "loud" enough to break through the inevitable clutter.

Operating communication channels also are excellent forums to promote On Strategy messages. Each function should issue every communication it produces in the context of the strategy message (the Conversation Platform). These include reporting documents, announcements, meetings, training, and other ongoing communication and activities. Simple modifications can go a long way in accomplishing this. For example, the finance department should organize reports and information around strategy. This might require only a slight adjustment, like adding a summary chart to the front page. On Strategy messages can be front and center in every meeting. One company we worked with, for example, had a primary focus on safety. They started every meeting, whether with two people or two thousand, with a message about safety. It was a little hokey when you're ready to start a meeting and someone takes a minute to point out the fire exits, but it was a good reminder of one of the nonnegotiables they valued. (Ford might have been less likely to produce the Pinto if they had started every meeting with a commitment to safety.) Training is another excellent operating channel for On Strategy messaging. Every training course should begin with an introduction about how the training supports the organization's strategy (why would the people be taking time off the job for training if it didn't support strategy?).

From a monthly operating review to a finance report to an employee newsletter, the opportunities to communicate On Strategy messages are everywhere.

To help identify the vehicles—traditional and operating—that are currently available, and to help identify where the organization needs additional vehicles, we've included a short list of the most common vehicles in Chapter Twelve. This Resource Guide also includes a brief overview of the most common work environments along with the communication opportunities and challenges each presents. It's important to be sensitive to the differences in those environments, as one vehicle rarely fits all. An assessment of the various environments in which your employee populations work will help determine which vehicles could be most effective.

The Conversation Platform as a Filter and Focus

The best way to focus a company's communication vehicles on strategy is to use the Conversation Platform as a filter and focus. Training all managers on the Conversation Platform helps reduce the babble in these communication pieces, as the managers work to communicate in support of the platform. Moreover, the communication and human resources departments should be very well versed in the platform, since those departments usually produce a lot of communication and manage the company's traditional vehicles.

Every article, video, town hall speech, and other communication from leadership should relate directly to explaining to employees what they need to do and should provide information and perspective about what they need to know and feel to take the right actions. Evaluating each communication as it relates to and supports the Conversation Platform will do that. If a communication isn't explaining to people what they are supposed to be doing or what they need to know and feel to take the right actions, why is it occupying space in leadership's communication channels?

Consider this requirement in all communication activities. For example, even one of the most mundane communication pieces—the personnel announcement—should be on strategy. The job of writing the personnel announcement is often a very unglamorous job pushed down to the junior staffer. But, depending on the situation, a personnel announcement can provide a great opportunity to reinforce behaviors your organization expects from its employees. To take advantage of that opportunity, ask this question: Is there any information we can provide through this communication that helps tell employees what they need to know or feel in order to take the right actions? In the personnel

> *The Conversation Platform and Action Equation provide a simple filter to help you ensure that all content is on strategy.*

announcement, for example, consider an organization that wants to promote risk taking in decisions. In this case, leaders want employees to know that they should take risks, and employees need to feel that leadership rewards risk taking. Therefore, a personnel announcement of a high-profile promotion should point out the risks the individual has taken, and the successes and even failures from which he or she has learned. This is one effective way to demonstrate to the organization that leadership values risk taking. It also gives managers and supervisors (the People Channel) an opportunity to talk with employees about the promotion and reinforce the desired behaviors.

This doesn't mean a company shouldn't communicate nice stories about how much money employees contributed to the United Way, recognize the employee of the month, or highlight a retiree who is engaged in wonderful community service. It also doesn't mean that HR should not report on benefits, or the technology department should not update people on developments in their area. But all these communications should relate to strategy. If they do not, and it's still deemed necessary to communicate them, make sure the priority is clear—it should appear not as the center spread of the newsletter, but perhaps as an article on the intranet home page. In this regard, it's wise to separate On Strategy communication from the more mundane information the company distributes. That way, employees know which vehicles are about strategy (and will help them do their jobs) and which focus more on the "nice to know."

Use Vehicles to Spark People Channel Conversations on Strategy

"Do you ever talk about the articles in the employee magazine with each other, or with your supervisor?" We ask that question every time we evaluate the effectiveness of traditional leadership communication channels, and the answer is seldom yes. If employees aren't talking about the information delivered through support channels—even if it's on strategy—you are missing a significant opportunity.

The difference between communication that sparks a conversation and one that doesn't is a matter of both content and style. People talk about things that are important to them. That's a given, and you address it by using the Action Equation as a filter for content. Leaders can add to the conversation, however, with communication that is controversial, provocative, or out of the ordinary.

Generate conversations in the workplace every day that can help employees understand and take action in support of strategy.

Formal leadership communication seldom exhibits these character-istics. In fact, many executives resist such material, and if they don't resist, others may. There usually is a process in companies to purge the controversial and provocative from general communication. This is all counterproductive.

Design and writing style are very important. There's certainly no single right way to design or write for a newsletter or produce a video or a poster. The culture of each organization often determines just how far you can go. But you should ask yourself, "Will this grab someone's attention or will he or she just pass it by?" The answer will vary in different environments. In an organization with a more conservative culture, it may not take much to get them to stop and look. Again, the purpose of the communication is not only to pres-ent information but also to spark conversations about it.

Take one of the most simple of communication vehicles: the poster. Many companies wallpaper their lobbies and hallways with posters of visions, values, and lame pictures of eagles soaring or the sun rising to try to illustrate what innovation, or focus, or commitment looks like. These posters seldom inform or motivate people, especially after they have been up for a few weeks—or years. Instead, put up posters that challenge people, make a controversial point, and jump out of the environment. Also, change the posters every few weeks, or don't bother putting them up (but give it a rest every two months or so). One orga-nization, for example, put up posters that depicted people reading the newspaper while ignoring poor-quality products moving down the line. The subtitle read, "That's not my job." Some employees recog-nized that was how the plant really operated—many employees didn't pay much attention to quality. Others got upset at the inference, pro-testing that they cared as much as management about quality. It all stirred up conversations—through which managers were able to make the point that the job rules in the plant set up just that kind of situa-tion, and quality suffered because of it (and the employees who were upset were made to recognize the problem as well). Bottom line: com-munication happened (and it would not have happened if the posters had been of Tiger Woods making flawless golf shots).

The need to embrace controversy becomes even more impor-tant when it involves difficult issues. We worked with one pharma-ceutical company, for example, that wanted to mobilize employees to support company efforts to address a growing belief among the public that drug companies used unethical practices in pricing and product testing. As part of the effort to inform and engage employees, the company launched a program whereby employees attended meetings at which leaders would discuss the issues. To be successful, the meetings had to spark interest and address issues head on, as opposed to the dry, apparently self-serving and one-sided presentation of information with which leadership often felt most comfortable. To this end, the producers of the meetings used media from popular culture—TV episodes or current films—as a springboard to engage and educate employees on issues.

It was a great communication opportunity that sparked considerable excitement and conversation within the organization. The challenge, however, was to follow through with the material. Executives bristled at the idea that such a controversial topic was on the agenda in the first place. The notion that the company would actually present to employees material that was critical of the industry, as depicted in popular television programs, floored them. Executives cut and cut until they had deleted most of the controversial material from the presentation. When producers suggested the company view the film *The Constant Gardener,* which dealt with unethical drug testing in a third-world country, the executives hit the ceiling.

Controversy about your company reaches and affects employees, whether you like it or not. Expect it and build on it. Don't avoid it. If employees are talking about a movie like *The Constant Gardener,* it makes no sense to avoid the topic. Instead, get in on the conversation. Expect that they will talk about provocative issues. Expect also that others—unions, activists, consumer groups, media, to name a few—will produce communication about your company and industry that will be controversial and provocative in nature. Ignoring it, and limiting your communication to the dry and mundane, limits your ability to lead your organization and your employees' ability to effectively engage in real conversations about your company and your industry. As you prepare On Strategy communication, if you don't think it will raise an eyebrow, produce a smile, or cause somebody to pause and think, go back to the drawing board and improve it. Give your employees something to talk about—on strategy.

Calendarize Communication Events

Leaders can anticipate communication opportunities and requirements, and they should commit those events to a calendar so they can use them in the communication drumbeat. This enables them to plan for them, commit the right resources, and put them in context with other events that affect employees. We use the term *communication events* in a very broad sense. A communication event is anything that will generate conversation among employees that will either enhance or reduce their ability or desire to execute strategy. Plan for these and leverage them in communication. Here are some of the communication events that leaders can use or must plan for:

- Earnings announcements
- Product launches
- Launch of new processes or systems to enable strategy execution
- New business win
- Publication of reports, such as the annual report or report on corporate responsibility
- Publication of analyst reports and earnings estimates
- Industry trend reports published by associations or the media
- Publication of industry and business lists, such as the Fortune 500 or Best Places to Work
- Customer events and news
- Regular competitor announcements, such as their earnings, surveys, and other material
- Company anniversaries
- Business cycles that affect employment, production, sales volume, and so on
- Government reports, such as economic forecasts and industry output
- Government-related events, such as congressional hearings and regulatory announcements
- Planned internal actions (even if planning is short term), such as personnel changes
- Scheduled communication, such as internal publications, conferences, and meetings
- Training schedules
- HR systems events, such as performance evaluations, employee surveys, and benefits changes
- Board of directors' meetings

- Internal reporting events, such as operating review meetings and budget reviews
- Leadership visits to operations
- Union events, such as elections and contract negotiations

Each of these is a potential communication event, and employee conversations about them are both opportunities and challenges. They can be opportunities if they show progress the organization is making against its goals. They may be challenges if the information presented could reduce confidence in strategies, conflict with what

Don't let any important communication opportunities pass you by. Plan and prepare for them.

management has said about strategy and performance, cause tension, or otherwise create misunderstandings among employees. Either way, these events will likely generate conversations, and leadership can influence those conversations by leveraging the People Channel. With the proper influence—by providing information that improves employee knowledge and understanding of strategy and their motivations to take action—leadership can use every communication event to drive action in support of strategy execution. Put them all on a calendar, plan for them, and communicate. This calendar forms the basis for annual communication planning concerning how to deliver the Action Equation and Conversation Platform to the organization.

TO RAISE THE VOLUME, RUN A CAMPAIGN

On Strategy communication is an ongoing discipline. Just like accounting, or finance, or process improvement, a leader can't start it, stop it, and start it up again without diminishing its utility and effectiveness. At the same time, there are instances in which leadership must turn up the volume on communication. These could be times of intense or specific change, when the company is under attack, or when the organization needs to rise to beat the competition.

In these situations, leadership can run a communication campaign that drives a higher level of information exchange and productive conversation. Campaigns involve greater frequency in pushing ideas and information through the People Channel and, in turn, greater support through traditional communication vehicles. Moreover, campaigns require greater visibility among top leadership.

Campaigns should fit into the overall communication scheme of the organization. In other words, they should be an extension and intensification of On Strategy communication, not a departure from strategy messaging. In that capacity, campaigns should have a beginning and an end—because a campaign puts greater pressure on leaders and the People Channel to communicate, and it is difficult to sustain over time. Moreover, employees tend to become immune to campaign tactics if they go on too long—in essence, the campaign just blends into the landscape and loses its effectiveness. Leaders do run successive campaigns, but it's most effective if they allow the organization to return to normal for a few months in between them.

> *Campaigns help turn up the volume during times that demand a special focus or intensified effort.*

We are not suggesting that communication starts and stops with campaigns. Leadership communication and the People Channel must be an ongoing part of running a business and executing strategy. Just as a company never stops executing strategy, leadership can never stop communicating and can never put the People Channel on hold. Campaigns simply raise the volume for a short period for a specific purpose. The following are some examples of communication campaigns designed to address a variety of business challenges.

Employee Brand Tour. One company engaged thousands of employees at its production facilities and corporate offices in a new brand rollout, and included events involving employees, families, community leaders, and customers. Employees saw previews of new advertising, experienced new products, and heard directly from customers. An aggressive internal communication campaign supported the events, with vehicles ranging from newsletters to the development of a music video representing the new brand. The tour generated the following results: 92 percent of employees felt increased pride; 79 percent felt an increased sense of belonging; 81 percent felt an increased sense of accomplishment; 71 percent felt more valued by the company; 77 percent felt an increased sense of teamwork; and 69 percent felt a greater sense of security.

Leadership Conferences. One company made a campaign out of a series of leadership conferences. The company held its first conference, and it was so successful the CEO decided to make it a biannual event. Every six months the leadership (approximately six hundred people) gathered over two days and shared strategic context and background for new brand and operating strategies. The conferences built understanding and excitement and equipped each attendee with a leadership tool kit to spread the message at office and operating locations.

Executive Face-to-Face Program. At one company, trust was the issue. Employees didn't trust management's intentions or capabilities, and therefore did not support a controversial new marketing strategy. To mend the relationship and build support, the executive team went on the road. Each of the top executives at the company visited at least one operational location every month. At each location, they had an open group Q&A session and walked the floor to talk one-on-one with employees on all shifts. Through the program, employees were able to get to know the "faceless name" at headquarters and understand in simple terms the reasons behind leadership decisions and how the employees could influence those decisions. The program resulted in an immediate increase in employee trust as measured by employee surveys.

Product Ride and Drive. The goal of this campaign was to get engineers not only informed about a new truck product design challenge, but also charged up to take new risks in their thinking. To "break the mold," engineers created a "ride and drive" program whereby the engineers were able to test drive not only their own products but also competitor models. Some of the engineers even used the trucks as their personal vehicles, which really gave them an idea of what customers faced every day on the job. The experience was an "Aha!" moment for the engineers that led to breakthrough design ideas.

Employee Celebration. In Chapter Seven we discussed an operation that was trying to avoid a unionizing attempt (which at initial stages was all but won by the union). Leadership drove its message home with a campaign designed to celebrate the independent-minded character of employees and appeal to their pride—the foundation of their Conversation Platform. Tools included leadership communication, supervisor communication training and messaging, posters, and bulletin board postings, to name a few. After the three-month campaign, culminating in an all-hands event, the company beat the union by a 3-to-1 vote.

Preparing Employees for Challenging News. A major kitchenware company had to cut its staff by 20 percent to reduce costs—a risky move in its emotionally charged direct-sales industry. Leadership navigated the issue head-on by raising, not lowering, the level of awareness of the layoffs. Departing employees were appreciated in three ways: through an extremely dignified, caring separation process; a special event at which all employees were able to mingle and talk; and an emotional but businesslike discussion with remaining employees emphasizing that the best way to appreciate departing employees was to make the company strong. It worked—morale (and sales) went up following the layoff.

Employee Issues Forums. We touched briefly in Chapter Four and earlier in this chapter on the challenges we faced with leadership of a pharmaceutical company when we recommended using media from popular culture—TV episodes or current films—as a platform to engage and educate employees on issues facing the health care industry. In the end, they bought in, and the team pulled off a great campaign. During a campus event, employees screened clips that vilified the industry and watched a panel discussion and Q&A with industry experts, company executives, and even critics. The company also launched a program that solicited personal essays or short videos on how medicines had personally affected employees' lives. The goal was to build employee pride and confidence in the industry as well as to expose employees to positive anecdotes about the value of medicine. The program created a buzz loud enough to attract a standing-room-only crowd to the launch event. Over 84 percent of the attendees found the event to be "greatly informative," 99 percent rated the overall event "excellent" or "good," and 94 percent of employees felt what they learned at the event would enable them to be a better ambassador of the company. One employee commented, "The public affairs programs do an excellent job of bringing these issues front and center. Then they provide information to combat the misinformation. Job well done!"

Defining the Brand. An equipment manufacturer was reinvigorating its position in the marketplace with new products and services, all revolving around a revitalized brand. Management looked at brand, however, as more than just what the company looked like, but also how it acted. That meant employees—from the manufacturing plant to sales people to customer service representatives—had to live the brand in their words and actions and at every point of customer contact. To make this happen, the company involved its employees in defining the brand itself (no one knows better than employees what our products are about, they suggested). Employees participated in focus groups and contributed to redefining the brand based on their experience with the product and customers. Employees know a few things about customers and the products they build for them—and leadership listened to them.

Training as an Event. One company made training around the Conversation Platform an event in itself. Executives and human resources and communications leaders selected and trained managers to deliver the training. A new manager-only communication channel was established with some fanfare. More than 306 managers and 138 communicators across the company experienced the training and changed how they communicated with employees and agents about strategy. Training evaluations showed that participants saw great value in the sessions. Feedback from the training included such comments as "The Conversation Platform is the most tangible progress I've seen so far toward the vision," "Keep the information coming," and "The Conversation Platform will be very useful."

HOW COMMUNICATION (THE FUNCTION) CAN HELP

Communication professionals are a valuable resource to increase the reach and effectiveness of leadership communication. Generally, they have control and input into the support vehicles. But they can be more than service providers—they can be counselors who contribute significantly as strategists and coaches.

We have worked with communication professionals and departments of all shapes and sizes. We've had the pleasure of working with fine, dedicated people—many of whom have contributed materially to the communication approach expressed in this book. As with any discipline, however, we've also worked with others not so well equipped. A leader has to know which group is available for support in order to understand how they can contribute.

If you have strategic communication professionals in your company, they will be rather obvious. In fact, they will be in your face. They will ask you what your strategies or business issues are, and they will tell you how communication can further your goals. They will work to drive business results—quality, productivity, brand delivery, cost, growth, profit—the same results that executive and line leadership focus on. They will continually challenge communication strategies and tactics to ensure they support business objectives. They will promote or kill communication initiatives based on their connections (or lack thereof) to strategy execution. They reject the idea that they provide a service to the organization: their contribution is strategic and critical. They challenge leaders on business principles and push them hard to conduct communication that gets business results.

If your communication function is tactical, its focus will be different. Tactically focused communication people ask you how communications can help, then do what you say (as if you are the communication expert). They focus on communication goals alone, such as awareness and understanding of information. They often view their jobs solely as producing communication—the company publication, the intranet, the town hall meeting, and other vehicles of communication. Sometimes these departments measure success against service metrics that focus on the number of engagements (speeches written, publications distributed), services provided, and client (executive) satisfaction. They may push leadership on narrow communication issues, but often don't have the confidence to challenge larger principles of business that relate to employee engagement and strategy execution. They are communication people, not business people.

Communication people of both types can be helpful to you. The former will help you develop effective leadership communication strategy and implement it. The latter will be useful in implementation—writing, designing communication vehicles, and the like. We recommend building the strategic communication capabilities of your organization. It will help deliver business results, and in the long term it will be more efficient. We offer the following steps to do so—and we suggest that many of these steps will also help tactical communication people do their jobs better.

Staff the Function to Drive Results

Placing the right people in the right positions is critical to the successful reinvention of a communication function. Operating managers tend to look at writing and verbal skills as key hiring criteria for communication professionals, as well as functional management capabilities and specific experience. These are important, but we believe the following competencies are what separate the strategic from the tactical:

Business acumen is critical to understanding strategy and the communication implications around it, and to winning the respect and trust of the organization. If communicators have a good understanding of how the company works, they will be able to counsel top management and provide value in the decision-making process. In this regard, we suggest finding communication experts who are also business people.

Bias for action is at the heart of strategic influence. Achieving results requires action. Communicators with a bias for action seize opportunities to make a difference in the company's performance. Look for a history of initiative and action—causes and effects—as opposed to a resume filled with activities.

Common sense is not as common as you'd think, as the old adage says. It is critical for strategic communication. Communicators who provide strategic influence must be able to look through the clutter of the workplace and their own biases to see the truth in a situation and the various realities affecting people. They must be able to quickly identify what will work at the earliest possible stage, separating fact from fancy, to provide management with effective counsel and influence their thinking at critical times. Life experience is more important than formal training in this regard.

Interpersonal savvy enables communicators to build trust and respect with the audiences they are addressing: frontline employees, business unit leaders, middle management, or senior management. The ability to understand the different realities of each of these groups and how to champion their perspectives and defuse high-tension situations is essential to success, as most business results are reached through compromise among varying viewpoints. Explore this competency with candidates and check them with references.

Positive attitude is defined as realistic optimism. It is not cheerleading or sugar-coating information. When leaders face a tough challenge, they know all too well what can go wrong. To them, finding solutions is much more valuable than issue identification. Communicators must see the opportunity in things more than the barriers to them, and they must have a bias toward taking action to make things happen. Tough challenges energize effective communication people and commit them to finding solutions.

Comfort around executives. The best communication professionals are comfortable around executive management and are willing to stand alone and bring truth to power. In other words, they tell leaders how it is—period. If communicators are to provide strategic counsel and earn a seat at the decision-making table, they must

Communicators with the right competencies can provide both strategic counsel and support to leaders.

have an ability to work one-on-one with leaders and feel comfortable enough to push back when leaders' ideas do not make sense.

Dealing with ambiguity is essential in today's rapidly changing business environment: as the saying goes, *those who do not change are left behind.* Successful characteristics for dealing with ambiguity include flexibility, the ability to shift gears comfortably, a level of comfort with risk taking, and the ability to effectively cope with change. As the company changes direction, so must its communication approach.

Strategic synthesis capability—the ability to "connect the dots"—is an essential competency in communication professionals. A key element of leadership communication is showing how everything fits together. This capability enables communication professionals to help you inform the Action Equation, develop the Conversation Platform, and produce meaningful ongoing communication.

Facilitation skills are also very helpful to leaders as they work through issues with their teams. A good facilitator can draw out information from employees, get it on the table for discussion, and help teams resolve problems. Few managers and supervisors are expert facilitators, so when they face difficult issues and controversy within their groups, a good facilitator from the communication department can be very valuable.

Passion for the job and the business is essential. Driving communication in an organization is a challenge. Every manager thinks he or she knows how to communicate, but most really don't. It takes some passion not only to work through the challenges that accompany communication (which are plentiful in themselves) but also to convince managers of the right way to communicate.

Set Expectations Related to Company Goals, Not Communication Goals

Every leader has a set of goals for which he or she is responsible. Those goals could concern cost, quality, customer satisfaction, production volume, increased sales—you name it. Communication professionals should be responsible for these same goals. This encourages them to think beyond traditional communication practices to develop ways in which communication can drive business results, not just communication results. This is critical when considering how communication can affect employee behavior—getting employees to do what you need them to—and in addressing root causes of behavior identified in the Behavior Chain.

Communication goals often revolve around awareness and understanding. As we've stressed throughout this book, many employees may both know what to do and understand why, yet still do nothing. In that event, employee survey scores on awareness and understanding could skyrocket, and it would appear that communication professionals have done their job well. In the final analysis, however, they've failed. It's like the old joke—the operation was a success but the patient died. If communication is great but nobody implements the strategy, is there really success?

When communication people have the same goals as leaders, it mitigates this kind of thinking and drives creativity and practicality. Once they are in the proverbial lifeboat with you, they row harder and with more discrimination. They will stretch their thinking about what communication can do to get business results, not just communication results. This philosophy will change the way the communication function thinks about itself, from staffing to the content of work to how the function is organized.

Involve Them Early

One of the most effective ways to leverage communication professionals is to involve them early in leadership processes, as you develop strategy and consider issues that affect employees. This way, they can contribute to strategy development. Communication professionals should be able to provide valuable insights into the mindset of employees, as well as identify hurdles that leadership may face in strategy execution.

We worked with one company, for example, that was considering building a large offshore facility as part of its strategy to reduce dependence on unionized domestic plants. Leaders of the communication department participated in the meetings in which leadership developed and debated strategy. They were deeply involved in a number of initiatives that involved union-represented employees, and they had conducted solid research on motivations and beliefs of those employees. Because of this knowledge, they raised issues regarding the strategy that leadership had not adequately contemplated. This included employees' inclination to support a strike in protest of the company's decision to build offshore plants. Because of this input, the company decided to build a smaller facility that was less threatening to the unions and represented employees. Operating management also launched a multiyear, focused business effort to build greater understanding among represented employees of the business issues and strategic necessities for the long-term viability of the company.

In this case, the decision making was at very high levels and in a critical situation. There are many decisions with various levels of risk in which communicators can participate to help run the business, while also building credibility to earn an invitation to help answer the critical questions surrounding decisions, such as these:

- As we consider our brand, can we be sure employees will deliver on the promises we make?

- Will employees support the new systems we want to implement, (such as supply chain, centralized services, and information sharing) so we realize the expected return on investment?

- Given employee relations, do we negotiate aggressive changes in the next union contract?

- Can we improve our quality and productivity in manufacturing by getting more out of our employees?

- Can we eliminate forced overtime to reduce absenteeism?

- Will a downsizing really net the savings we expect?

- Can we get the synergies we expect from this acquisition?

- Before we commit financial goals to Wall Street, are we confident we're getting the full performance story from our organization?

Involving communication professionals early in the strategic development process also will equip them better at a tactical level— when it is time to communicate to the organization. The difference between an informed and involved counselor or communicator and one brought in at the last minute is immense, as are the results either one can produce. This is particularly true in message development and regarding integration of communication processes and vehicles. It takes time and planning to infuse leadership's message in the formal communication channels a company may have, and even more time to consider the informal channels. This is particularly the case when the communication people do not control the channels, such as functional meetings, planning sessions, and the like.

Involve Them Deeply—and Prioritize

In addition to early involvement, communication professionals are more effective when they are deeply involved in business planning and decision making. That means making a communication professional an integral part of the various teams formed to drive initiatives forward, not a part-time adjunct. In the example just discussed, the communication professionals influenced the size of an offshore production facility. They were able to do that because they were full members of the strategy-planning group. That group met every Saturday for more than six months, and the communication professionals were at every meeting. They were involved in interim meetings with other functions as they investigated alternative strategy options, they prepared communication-related recommendations for the larger group's consideration, and they had access to the CEO to discuss strategy development. In short, communication leadership was part of the strategy planning process, not an afterthought brought into the process when leadership was getting ready to communicate.

This level of involvement can be a challenge. As in any function, the number of communication people is limited, and the number of initiatives a company undertakes usually exceeds that total. Communication resources should be allocated to the areas of greatest need.

Moreover, executive and line management often treat communication people as a service resource. For example, because they write well, communicators may be expected to help produce a memo or speech for a business leader's department (or for the leader personally, if that person is a senior executive). The communication function also tends to become responsible for miscellaneous activities loosely associated with communication, such as conducting the company holiday party, the United Way campaign, and so on. Unless you have unlimited resources, this is not the best way to utilize your communication professionals. Just as the finance department would rebel if people continually asked them to add up their expense reports for them, the role of communication professionals should not be to put presentations into PowerPoint, create trinkets, or manage parties. If an executive needs a speech, the communication people should write it *if* it serves the strategic communication needs of the organization—in other words, if it is part of a larger communication effort to drive business results. If the company needs a writer's bureau to support executives or managers, or a party- and meeting-planning unit, it should create or outsource them. But these are not leadership communication activities unless they are about strategy.

SUMMARY

Once you have informed the Action Equation, built a Conversation Platform, trained and equipped your managers, and launched the People Channel, it is time to kick-start communication and step on the gas. This happens through the various communication channels available in most organizations, which include traditional communication vehicles—such as the company newsletter, intranet, and town hall meetings—as well as the operating vehicles that managers and supervisors use to run the business, such as departmental meetings, reporting documents, memos, and email.

To communicate on strategy, you can use these vehicles to produce a continuous drumbeat of information about strategy (based on the Conversation Platform) and occasional campaigns that turn up the volume of communication for specific, short-term purposes. You can create a drumbeat by keeping the content of every vehicle related to and in support of strategy. Even simple communication such as a personnel announcement can contribute to the drumbeat and reinforce the Conversation Platform. By setting up a communication calendar to track all of the organization's happenings that are communication events, you can use every opportunity to its fullest.

As you create the drumbeat, it's important to use communication that generates conversation by its nature—communication that has some level of controversy or is provocative, not the normal fare. The On Strategy approach is an ongoing conversation with employees, not a monologue, and the best vehicles generate and promote that conversation.

The communication department is a valuable resource in delivering On Strategy communication and achieving business results if you establish and use it strategically. It's best to populate the communication function with people who are both good business people and passionate about communication. The combination can be very powerful in driving new thinking about the role communication plays and how leaders use communication to deliver business results. Communication people also provide valuable tactical support in delivering communication. To make the most of your communication people, you should involve them in the entire process of strategy development, so they can contribute to and understand strategy in the deepest ways. Prioritizing their work allows them to concentrate on strategic essentials as opposed to providing communication support and services. Tying their growth and compensation to business results, rather than intermediary communication results or the production of materials, puts them in the lifeboat with you, where they belong and can help the most.

CHAPTER ELEVEN

You: The Top Leader's Role

T he People Channel is the sum of its parts: all of the managers and supervisors up and down the leadership ranks and informal leaders in and out of management. Its effectiveness is a direct result of top leadership's commitment to it. The People Channel spreads the responsibility for strategic communication across all leaders, thereby making communication more effective and less of a burden on top leadership. However, the top leader's role is indispensable in forming, shaping, and sustaining the People Channel. In that role, top leaders must manage the People Channel, beginning with setting high expectations.

EXPECT A LOT

We recently worked with a company that needed to share important news with its employees and wanted a process to ensure that the communication was effective. They proposed holding a town hall meeting with all employees live at corporate headquarters and with regional locations linking in through video conferencing. We suggested providing managers across the company with a tool kit to support them in facilitating follow-up conversations with their teams. Their response was, "We've tried that before. We make presentations available to managers on the intranet, but nobody really does anything with them." We asked, "What did you expect?"

We weren't trying to be glib. Leaders get what they expect in any endeavor, including communication and participation in the People Channel. You must aggressively communicate those expectations, monitor execution on an ongoing basis, and keep the need to communicate among the top priorities you pursue.

Never Assume and Always Monitor

You must outline the specific actions you expect managers to take at every communication juncture. The communication calendar suggested in Chapter Ten can serve as a guide to prompt top leaders to remind the managers of their responsibilities. Especially when first implementing the People Channel, it's critical to tell managers what you want them to do, how, and when. Also, explain why it's important. Tell them every time—past the point where it seems annoying and repetitive. Then check on their response. If it is inadequate, demand better. Consider the following example:

A CEO was implementing a new process for communicating strategy. He held meetings with the company's director-level managers, and told them he expected that group to communicate to their respective teams with a sense of urgency. When he checked on progress, he found that the first meeting the directors had set up was six weeks after his initial presentation. That's not an urgent response. He needed to demand better—for two reasons. First, the organization needed the information in order to be able to deliver results. Second, allowing the time lag spoke volumes about the importance of the communication. He wouldn't wait six weeks for managers to communicate a reorganization or even a new expense account policy. Six weeks shouldn't be acceptable for communication on strategy, either.

The CEO wisely put in place a method to measure the impact of the strategy communication—an electronic survey of all employees, segmented into departments and levels. We recommended that he conduct the survey in six weeks and tell his leadership group that individual managers would be held accountable for improved results. By doing so, the CEO set an expectation

Never assume leaders know what's expected of them. Make it clear, and follow up.

that the process would be *complete* in six weeks, not just starting. That was the sense of urgency he wanted.

It's important to be specific about expectations for each major communication action. For example, if you are providing an update on your organization's performance and want managers to first attend a meeting with you to review, then sit down with their employees in small groups to review and discuss the information, tell them that. Don't assume they know what the next steps are just because you've done it a certain way in the past. Accompany each major communication opportunity with a clear set of expectations, as well as a process to determine whether or not managers and supervisors meet those expectations.

Orchestrate Communication Delivery

In addition to setting expectations for major communication events, top leadership also must manage the overall People Channel process and orchestrate the campaigns required to drive On Strategy communication. Leaders can delegate some of the day-to-day work involved in managing and orchestrating communication execution. The communication function can be instrumental in this role (particularly if the principles of communication functions outlined in Chapter Ten are observed). At the same time, top leaders must play an active, visible role in managing the People Channel. That involves establishing measurements, allocating resources, recognizing good communication performance, and making communication a priority task, not only for the organization, but also for you.

MEASUREMENT

The ultimate measurement tools are your business metrics. Communication should influence results, or it will not (and should not) be a priority. That makes sense. Leaders from the top of the organization to the bottom are ultimately responsible for making and selling products and services. They should pay the most attention to those activities that help them make and sell products and services better, faster, less expensively, at higher quality—whichever outcomes are most important to the organization. When measuring communication and holding managers and supervisors accountable for improvement, there must be an undeniable connection between communication and business results. Otherwise, line management eventually will relegate communication to a position of secondary priority.

In fact, we don't recommend holding managers accountable for communication metrics unless it is clear that (1) communication has a demonstrable impact on results, and (2) the organization believes it. This is different from the approach that many companies pursue, which often involves measuring manager communication through results of an employee survey. Holding a manager accountable for communication metrics (such as employee awareness and understanding of strategy) when there is no clear connection to results is often counterproductive. First, communication becomes just another job managers have to do, not a *way* to do their jobs. Busy managers resent more work that seems secondary to their primary jobs, and they will find ways to avoid it. Indeed, if managers come to believe that they are responsible for improving the specific, communication-related scores on the survey, which are not connected to the operating results for which they are responsible, they become distracted from real business results—quality, cost, customer satisfaction, and so on. That's not productive.

Keep leaders focused on metrics that matter. Help them see that leadership communication helps them do their jobs—it doesn't give them another one.

The two most effective ways we've found to connect On Strategy communication to business results is through research that (1) shows causal linkages between the two and/or (2) demonstrates the quality and effectiveness of information flow within an organization.

Relate Communication to Performance Metrics

If we told a line supervisor we could guarantee millions of dollars in quality improvements simply by holding a ten-minute meeting every day, most would jump at the chance. In some situations, it's possible to measure communication effectiveness, as well as the impact communication has on business metrics, in such a way. This requires a highly structured environment in which metrics are tracked diligently and consistently. In such situations, researchers can use hierarchal linear modeling to determine the causal linkages between observable communication behaviors and specific business results.

For example, we used this research approach in a manufacturing plant to identify how communication could improve quality and productivity. The survey, designed by Employee Motivation & Performance Assessment, Inc., asked employees a short set of questions about topics including communication, management style, and teamwork. The communication questions focused on very specific supervisory behaviors, such as "My supervisor provides me with the information I need to do my job." The results of the survey, organized by department and level, compared communication performance with operating metrics such as defect rates, lost-time accidents, overtime, and production volume. Through hierarchical linear modeling, the research predicted improved performance through improved communication (the foundation of which was departmental meetings).

For example, for every point improvement in the overall communication score posted in the survey, the research predicted an approximate 20-percent decrease in defect rates per thousand. Leadership repeated the survey nine

Don't buy into the myth that you can't measure the impact of communication. In the right environment, you can measure causal linkages between communication and business metrics.

months later and after leaders had put communication tools and processes in place. Defect rates declined, as predicted by the survey.

This research was powerful in two ways. First, it showed that communication was important to operating performance, and it drew the attention of leadership throughout the plant. Second, it helped managers and supervisors do their jobs: producing quality products. The research demonstrated that improving communication was a path to improving performance that could be evaluated against other options—such as investment in training, equipment, and the like—because the research enabled the calculation of a concrete return on investment provided by communication. As a result, plant management from top to bottom embraced communication as an operating strategy and continually implemented improvements in communication approaches.

Measure Information Flow

We have yet to find a senior leader, manager, supervisor, or line employee who disagrees with the fact that people need information to do their jobs, and that the timeliness, quality, and completeness of that information affects business results. People universally embrace this connection. As one manager put it, "You can't do a good job without good information. It's undeniable." They get it.

Therefore, measuring information flow within an organization is an effective way to measure managerial performance around communication. It provides an excellent look into an organization's management style and culture. From how people share information, we can see how they include others in decision-making processes, communicate with candor (or not), deal with difficult issues, work through formal or informal structures, share information important to their jobs, and maintain a strategic focus. Moreover, information flow is a benign organizational attribute that does not threaten managers as might an assessment that directly measures personal style and management credibility. The research we have conducted considers twelve specific attributes of information flow as outlined in Table 11.1 (which were used to identify the five communication profiles discussed in Chapter One). Such research provides a benchmark to evaluate managers and their progress in improving communication (as defined by information flow). It also provides a starting point to delve deeper into information flow issues that can create barriers to performance. Both discussion groups (as described in Chapters Five and Six) and one-on-one interviews can help surface the underlying issues behind poor movement of information within an organization.

Communication is a means to get business results, not a result in itself. At the same time, it is reasonable to expect managers to implement communication processes and to measure whether they do it effectively or not. These are concrete actions, which are observable and measurable. For example, after a leader holds a town hall meeting with all employees and asks managers to hold follow-up conversations with their teams, it's reasonable (and preferable) to follow up to ensure that those meetings are held. Over the long term, however, it is most effective to relate that action to delivering specific results. Research methods using hierarchical linear modeling, or information flow research, make that connection. That way, leaders up and down the organization recognize communication as part of the job, not another job to do.

Attribute	Description
Movement Up	The extent to which communication moves up the organization hierarchy. Low scores are associated with isolated bosses and low interaction among the levels of an organization.
Movement Down	The extent to which communication moves down through an organizational hierarchy. Low scores are associated with isolated frontline staff.
Movement Across	The extent to which communication moves across lateral borders (such as between departments or divisions) in the organization. Low scores are associated with difficult-to-penetrate silos in the workplace.
Timeliness	The extent to which communication arrives on time. Low scores are associated with information arriving chronically late or outside its window of usefulness.
Completeness	The extent to which all crucial information is conveyed. Low scores are associated with information that omits key elements so that critical details or important implications are lost.
Inclusiveness	The extent to which crucial employees are included in the exchange of information about decisions that concern them. Low scores indicate that critical employees are being excluded during decision making.
Infrastructure	The extent to which systems and processes are used as reliable and helpful sources of information. Low scores indicate problems in the communication (management) process used by employees.
Dialogue	The extent to which communication is an exchange in which people speak and listen in a genuine, constructive fashion. Low scores are associated with a lack of in-depth collaboration and consideration of information.
Candor	The extent to which communication tells the truth. Low scores are associated with censoring and stretching the truth, either for personal reasons or reasons that concern office politics.
Relevance	The extent to which communication sticks to the pertinent topic at hand. Low scores are associated with organizations that either have lost their focus or have little notion of who does what inside the company.
Motives	The extent to which communication is tactful, insightful, and compelling. Low scores are associated with communication whose primary motive is to punish, to instill a sense of fear, or to intimidate dissenters.
Strategic Direction	The extent to which information is communicated in the context of the company's strategic plans, so that employees can synthesize disparate and complex information from multiple sources. Low scores are associated with poorly articulated or communicated direction to the organization.

Table 11.1. Twelve Attributes of Information Flow.

REWARD, RECOGNIZE, AND HOLD ACCOUNTABLE

As in all performance-related situations, it is important to follow up with employees with the proper rewards, encouragement, and reinforcement. Communication is no different, so it is important to recognize managers who are setting an outstanding example. If appropriate, make recognition as public as possible to demonstrate the importance of communication to the rest of the organization. For example, at one company a key strategy was to make it easier for customers to do business with the company. Senior executives were confident that employees on the front line had great ideas on how they could further that strategy, and they asked managers to have conversations with employees to encourage them to share their ideas. One manager took the assignment very seriously and not only encouraged employees to identify what their team could do to make it easier for customers to do business with the company, but also helped them bring many of their ideas to life. Top leadership personally recognized the manager with a pat on the back (literally) and a feature story in the company's monthly newsletter. The article recognized the individuals and their teams as well as the impressive actions the manager took to implement those ideas.

Make it clear. Leaders are expected to actively participate in this new communication system and will be rewarded and disciplined accordingly.

On the other hand, it's equally important to discipline managers who don't exhibit the communication behaviors that leaders are asking of them. This is important even if the managers are achieving short-term business results. We often see top leaders promote managers who are poor communicators and who ignore their responsibilities as part of the People Channel, just because they are nevertheless delivering short-term results. Such promotions are counterproductive for the long term. Eventually, poor communication catches up to those managers, especially when they move into positions that require leading larger groups of people. Effective communication is not an option; it is a necessity. Rewards, recognition, and leadership selection criteria must reflect that.

PRIORITIZE

Beyond managing the People Channel, a leader must also manage his or her own communication focus and activity. This begins with prioritizing where the leader spends time and resources. We believe that leaders must set communication priorities based on business needs. You can set these priorities by looking at the most important things the organization must accomplish and comparing those demands against the communication effectiveness of the people responsible for implementing the programs. If managers, departments, or functions that are ineffective at communication are responsible for implementing high-priority tasks, leaders must intervene. One way to set these priorities is to use the measurement tools just described to identify underperforming communicators, then match those against priority initiatives and chart the risks, as illustrated in Figure 11.1.

In this case, the senior leader's priorities become clear. A functional silo (A) responsible for a high-priority project is suffering from severe information flow problems. The top leader must intervene to prevent problems associated with information flow. Another

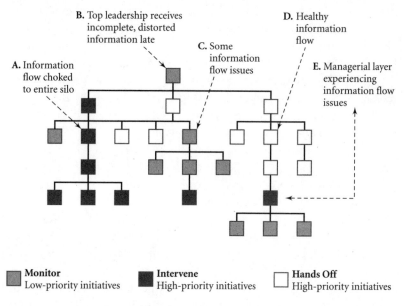

Figure 11.1.   Identifying Communication Priorities.

situation (E) involves a manager who is choking information flow and has an impact on the ability of other functions to get their jobs done. Helping this manager improve information flow also must be a priority. A third situation (C) involves a silo that is experiencing some information flow problems. Their work, however, is not strategically critical. In this case, the senior leader can monitor the situation, attend to it later, or delegate authority to correct the problems. Another functional group (D) is also expected to deliver a high-priority project, but is functioning well from an information flow standpoint. In that case, the top leader can take a hands-off approach. Addressing information flow priorities in this way will help improve results, and also improve information flow to the senior leader (B), which is usually important for that person's decision-making ability (and ability to sleep at night).

LEAD BY EXAMPLE

As leaders set expectations for the People Channel, managers in the channel will set expectations for top leadership. This includes, for example, a commitment to prepare them through the Conversation Platform training, as well as a commitment that top leaders will keep managers in the communication loop. Top leadership also must provide clear and consistent alignment at the top of the organization. Few things are more likely to discourage a manager from communicating with his or her employees than confusing and contradictory messages from leadership. Leadership's commitment to the People Channel is particularly important when managers believe they are putting themselves at risk by positioning themselves as a reliable source of information or as a channel through which to provide feedback and insights. For example, in the past they might have made promises they later could not keep to their employees about information because leaders above them did not deliver.

Equally critical to these requirements is the commitment top leaders must make to fulfill their role as a communicator. A leader sets the tone and expectation around communication with his or her words *and* actions. If others in the organization see the senior leader (and the leader's group) communicating openly and frequently with the organization, they will be more likely to follow suit. This takes time and energy, and the best leaders deliver.

Moreover, there are times when only the top leader will do. We worked with a CEO who bristled at spending time on communication,

Your commitment to communication, demonstrated through words and actions, sets the tone for the entire organization.

despite the fact that one of the key employee motivational issues facing the organization was a lack of trust in his intentions and abilities. When a leader needs to build trust, shore up confidence, or simply show employees he or she cares, there's no substitute for face-to-face communication.

We can think of few examples that better demonstrate the requirements of leadership communication for a CEO than the experience of General Dwight Eisenhower during the six months before the D-Day invasion. We can find no parallel of equal intensity in business, and few leaders who have fulfilled their responsibilities with more dedication and effectiveness.

General Eisenhower was one of the busiest people in the world from January to June 1944. He was orchestrating the largest movement of people and equipment in history. His organization was going to ferry the equivalent of a midsized city across a body of water—while people were shooting at them. His "board of directors"—Franklin Roosevelt, Winston Churchill, and Joseph Stalin—couldn't have been more demanding. Eighteen-hour days were typical, and he took only one day off: Tuesday, April 4. Despite these crushing responsibilities, he always carved out significant time to communicate to his troops.

Eisenhower understood that the success of the operation, and ultimately the war, lay in the hands of the individual rifleman. Therefore, he made a concerted effort to spend as much time with the troops as possible. He knew that only his genuine concern would garner the confidence and respect of the soldiers and people back home that was essential to success. In the 142 days from January 15 to June 6, 1944, he spent 34 days in some formal contact with frontline troops—nearly 25 percent of his time. That doesn't include his travel time to meet with the troops, time spent on public appearances and media broadcasts, or impromptu visits with those soldiers.

We suggest that any leader questioning whether leadership communication is necessary should consider Eisenhower's commitment. Sometimes, as was true for Ike, no one else can fill your shoes. When that's the case, suck it up and make it happen. That's what separates the great leaders from all the rest.

CHAPTER TWELVE

"How to" Resource Guide

T hroughout the book, we refer to a number of processes that help leaders and people in communication or human resources get information, process it, and then communicate it. Our purpose in *Beyond the Babble* is not to provide detailed tools on how to gather information, conduct meetings, produce communication vehicles, and the like. There are already some very good books on these subjects by experts who know more about each than we do. That said, we have developed some approaches that work very well for us and are easy to implement; you may find them valuable. We offer these "how to" processes in this chapter.

CONDUCTING DISCUSSION GROUPS

We suggest using discussion groups as a research tool on a frequent and ongoing basis (so long as you do something about the findings and tell employees that you did). Discussion groups resemble, to some degree, the focus groups that research organizations conduct, but they are not as structured and aren't held before two-way mirrors, nor are they videotaped or recorded (employees tend to clam up when they feel they are being interrogated). In turn, they are not as expensive or intrusive to the organization. Ideally, discussion groups are small gatherings of employees that delve into some very simple but revealing topic areas. You may feel it's unnecessary to use a process simply to talk to employees you work with every day, but we assure you it works. We're always amazed with what we find out from discussion groups—it's time well spent.

The following is a process for holding discussion groups that you can apply as needed, with variations depending on the specific situation.

Use a Facilitator, if at All Possible

To lead the groups, it usually makes sense to use a third-party facilitator from outside your direct business or organization. An unbiased party helps to encourage dialogue that is more open. Also, a facilitator has broader permission to ask difficult questions and dig deeper than does someone directly involved with the group who may have current or future interaction with the employees. Moreover, an experienced facilitator can quickly build rapport with the group and help make them comfortable speaking about difficult topics. It's also important to have an assistant to take notes, so the facilitator can focus on developing the conversation. The discussion groups should be just that—an opportunity to engage employees in a discussion. Therefore, you need to make every effort to put the employees at ease.

Designing Discussion Groups

Once you decide you want to conduct discussion groups, it's important to design them properly. Start by identifying the group of employees from whom you need to hear. Depending on the goal of the discussion groups, you may need to hear from a cross section of the entire organization or employees in just one business or function. If, for example, the goal is to better understand the motivational connections of employees across the business, then it's important to consider the possibility that there are subgroups of employees with different experiences, and each of those subgroups needs to be represented. To do this, look at your organization, consider how it was formed and how it grew, and identify distinct groups with similar histories and associations. For example, you may have office employees and manufacturing employees; if so, you probably need to hold discussion groups with each. You may have headquarters employees and field employees. Again, hold discussions with each. Many companies have a significant percentage of employees who have been at the company for a while as well as a new population hired more recently. More than likely their experiences differ, so separate discussion groups would be appropriate. Finally, many disconnects happen when companies grow through acquisition: the organization is composed of employee groups with different histories, so discussion groups with each of them could be particularly revealing.

We recommend keeping the various employee subsets in separate discussion groups because people talk more when they support each other in their discussions rather than conflict with each other. Moreover, many employees won't speak openly in front of superiors. As resource and time limitations are nearly always a factor, it's better to have a smaller number of groups in which conversation is robust rather than a large number of groups in which people will stay quiet. We recommend five to seven people in a group; this is a manageable size that promotes conversation. Much of the richness of the discussion groups comes from the conversations sparked between employees, so groups of just two or three employees don't usually provide enough opportunity for dialogue, and groups larger than seven or eight get a little unwieldy.

We're often asked, "How many employees do I need to talk to?" Unfortunately, there is no magic number. You will most likely be able to identify the motivational connections employees have with the organization if you assemble ten groups or fewer. More often than not (except in the case of acquisitions), organizations are composed of people who think alike. People tend to hire people like themselves, and when people work side by side for some time, they begin to assume a group personality. As a result, the makeup of your organization will drive the number of groups more than its size. For example, we identified the motivational trigger of a company with one hundred thousand employees by conducting fewer than six groups—the employees were very similar in their experiences. At another company, with only seven thousand employees, we conducted more than ten groups, but because those employees experienced different histories, we were still somewhat uncertain of the total picture. Just talk to as many groups as necessary to get the information you need. Once the groups get repetitive, stop.

Executing Discussion Groups

A good way to kick off a discussion group is to create a common understanding of what holding the groups will accomplish and to share some ground rules. We suggest starting the groups with a brief discussion around the following statements:

- We're holding several discussions just like these with groups of employees across the company.
- All we're asking of you is to be candid and share your thoughts openly.
- We will take notes so we can identify the common themes after all the sessions are completed; however, we will not attribute any specific comments to any one person in particular.

To get employees comfortable talking, ask everyone to introduce themselves with their name, position, how long they've been with the company, and why they joined in the first place. The discussion leader should listen to everybody and not judge in any form or fashion. From the outset, it must be clear to employees that the discussion is about listening to them and nothing else. The discussion follows a set of questions designed to get employees talking about a particular issue.

In the course of the discussion groups, employees will cover a wide range of topics. An effective facilitator will help keep them on track, but it's also important to let employees ramble and talk. It's more likely the discussion will result in meaningful information that way. Interpreting all that talk can be a challenge, however. Here are a few tips:

- Look for overall *themes.* These are the topics that the discussions seem to gravitate to and return to, or to which several people contribute with some level of energy. Don't simply count the number of statements, however, in order to interpret the relative strength of various positions. Intensity is just as important as quantity in evaluating the importance of what employees discuss.
- Identify which themes shift between groups and segments, and which themes hold true for all groups. This will be helpful in creating common messages and communication and identifying where you may have to alter your approach.
- Look at the topics to which employees devote most of their energy. For example, in a discussion group designed to surface

motivation, if employees talk a lot about customers, it indicates a connection to customers. If they talk a lot about working with other people, it indicates employees place a lot of value on teamwork and each other. These are good indicators of the "why" that motivates them.

- Notice what employees don't say as well as what they do say. If topics such as the customer or product do not come up, it means employees aren't connected to those parts of the company.

- Evaluate the outliers—groups that are at odds with the rest of the organization. Is there an explanation for it? Is it an anomaly driven by local issues or experiences?

Insights and learnings from employee discussion groups can be powerful inputs to On Strategy communication. The more the organization gets used to and comfortable participating in such discussions, the richer the output.

Discussion Groups to Identify Motivational Connections

Discussion groups held specifically to identify employee motivational connections must be conducted in a very relaxed atmosphere. Allow employees to think about questions, and let discussion wander as employees consider the questions. It is important that they realize there are no wrong answers to any of the questions. These are the motivations employees have, not necessarily the motivations the company would like them to have. They are intrinsic—and not the result of company reward and recognition programs. The following are some questions we have found effective in identifying motivational connections:

- What brought you to this company when you joined? Why do you stay?

- If a good friend of yours asked about joining your company or group, what would you tell them that would attract them to join?

- What inspires you in your work? What gets you out of bed in the morning?

- What do you believe is unique about this company relative to its competitors?
- Does the reason you came to work here still exist today and hold true? In what way? How do you see it expressed—experience it?
- Finish this sentence for me: "This place is a great place to work because . . ."
- When you have a really great day, what does it look like?
- If you had to choose one word to describe your company, what would it be?
- If you were to give your company an award for something, what would it be?
- If you could keep just one thing true about this company into the future, what would it be?

We provide these questions only as a guideline to generate discussion. It's not necessary to ask all of them or to get answers to all of them. If the course of the conversation takes an entirely different path, that's okay, as long as people are talking about what connects them to the company and their work at an emotional level. We held one discussion group, for example, in which we outlined why we were meeting and asked for introductions, and that was it. We didn't say another word. Two hours later, employees stopped talking and asked if we had any more questions. We didn't—they had said all we needed to hear.

Once you identify the motivational connection, bounce it off a few "informal" leaders you respect and who have their hand on the pulse of the organization. (We talk more about informal leaders in Chapter Eight.) Explain to them what you're trying to understand and what you believe you heard the employees say. This follow-up, in addition to providing greater perspective, will confirm or challenge the output of the discussion groups and help determine whether more research is necessary. Consider, however, that discussion groups, by their design, do not provide incontrovertible statements about the motivations of employees; rather, they are an indication of what makes them tick. This is as much art as science, so your understanding of your employees will evolve as you become more sensitive to it. The discussion groups are an important first step in this process.

Discussion Groups to Inform the Behavior Chain

Discussion groups are an excellent way to identify the experiences and beliefs—the "why nots"—of the Behavior Chain we discuss in Chapter Six. When digging for the "why nots," it's even more important to have an impartial facilitator, particularly when the experiences involve management issues around commitment, competency, or trust. It also is especially important for the facilitator to stress the anonymity of the discussion groups—confirming that management will not be able to trace statements back to employees. Finally, carefully consider the makeup of the groups so employees will feel free to talk. Frontline employees may not be forthcoming in front of managers or informal leaders aligned with management. With that in mind, we recommend the following questions to generate a productive conversation around employee experiences that affect their beliefs and behaviors:

- What's different today, if anything, from when you joined the company?
- Has the reason you joined the company been maintained over time? If not, what specific actions or experiences caused the change?
- What kinds of things take the steam out of you—your motivation?
- Finish this sentence for me: "This place is a frustrating place to work because . . ."
- What makes working here hard?
- If a good friend were to ask you about joining the company, what kind of warnings would you give them for them to consider?
- When you have a really tough, frustrating day, what does it look like?
- What stands in the way of you being able to do your best?
- What's your understanding of what's expected of you, and is that expectation reasonable?
- When you have done what management has asked in the past, what has happened?

THE MEMORY GAME

You can't communicate it if you can't remember it. That seems like a no-brainer, but we're often surprised at how leaders ignore this simple concept. They just feel compelled to include too much in their messaging. To clarify, we don't mean to suggest you hide information from employees or make it difficult for them to get it; rather, we are suggesting that the messages leadership conveys should be simple, but constructed so the messages create a pathway to everything employees need and want to know. They also have to be concise, so that people—both the managers and supervisors delivering them and the employees hearing them—can remember them and have conversations about them in the moment. That means information has to be organized into no more than about five chunks.

To convince a leader who is reluctant to simplify his or her messages, try this simple memory game. It's an experience that changes a lot of minds, and it takes only a few minutes. There are three successive games or tests, shown in Table 12.1. They involve your reading a list of words at about one-second intervals. People listen to you, but

Test One	Test Two	Test Three
Read the list with one-second intervals between the words. When you have completed the list, ask employees to write down the words they remember.	Repeat the same process as in Test One.	Repeat the process, except this time, before asking them to write the words, ask them to count backward from the number 18 in intervals of three (18, 15, 12 . . .)
North . . . apple . . . John . . . red . . . dime . . . pear . . . Bill . . . blue . . . quarter . . . West . . . dollar . . . South . . . grape . . . nickel . . . yellow . . . East . . . green . . . Robert . . . banana . . . Charlie	bream . . . later . . . pot . . . start . . . job . . . clog . . . mayor . . . else . . . wage . . . jowl . . . chap . . . trout . . . lot . . . tape . . . dusk . . . wreak . . . list . . . smug . . . duck . . . big	time . . . stab . . . solve . . . house . . . mutt . . . draft . . . say . . . off . . . royal . . . court . . . slot . . . hand . . . dirt . . . plot . . . out . . . greet . . . dent . . . stale . . . stone . . . dice

Table 12.1.   The Memory Game.

Source: Human Memory, "Exploring Human Memory: Experiment 1," http://human-factors.arc.nasa.gov/cognition/tutorials/ModelOf/index.html.

are instructed not to write down any words until you say so. When you finish reading the first list, ask people to write down the words they remember. Do the same for the second list. Then do the same for the third list, but this time after you complete the list ask participants to count backward by threes from eighteen, then write down the words they remember. Watch people struggle to remember, and then point out that it's even harder in a noisy plant or when employees are pressuring you for answers.

In our experience with Test One, people remember from thirteen to eighteen words. In Test Two, they remember from three to eight words. And in Test Three they remember fewer yet. These results are similar to those posted in memory research studies. This simple test reveals a few important insights relevant to leadership communication (in addition to the fact that memory is limited):

- People can remember more when the material is linked together. People scored higher in Test One because they were able to group the words into five categories: colors, directions, names, fruits, and money. They still remembered only five chunks, but the chunks contained more than one word.

- In Tests Two and Three, the words listed had no relationship to each other, so they couldn't be grouped together; thus participants remembered less.

- People remember less when the material is unfamiliar or they are distracted, which also explains the lower results in Tests Two and Three.

ALIGNMENT INTERVIEWS AND SNAPSHOT

It can be a challenge to get senior leaders to talk openly when they disagree with each other—particularly in a group. We've been successful drawing out very controversial information and then generating productive dialogue about it, through a two-step process. Step One involves interviewing the leaders involved, one-on-one, with a series of questions designed to get them talking. Step Two brings those executives together and uses their words (played back anonymously) to generate conversation about difficult topics.

Here's how to implement this approach to put tough issues on the table so leaders discuss and resolve them. We recommend this process for teams in which people generally respect each other and team politics are not the driving motivation among members. Also, the leader of the team must be ready and willing to listen, consider options, and participate. This process is less effective in highly dysfunctional teams; for those, we recommend more intensive team intervention as often provided by human resources or organizational development people.

To begin the process, set up one-on-one interviews with the leaders involved. It's best to use a third-party facilitator—somebody people will trust. Try to interview all the leaders; if that's not possible, include a good cross section of people so most, if not all, views are represented. In those meetings, explain that the information you are asking about will be held anonymous but will be used to put various issues on the table for discussion. You will protect their names and contributions by editing comments to make them anonymous, then mixing them together with comments others made. Stress to interviewees, however, that you will communicate the messages without altering them—their words will not be distorted.

If you are seeking alignment around strategic direction, the Conversation Platform and the Action Equation are good places to start the conversation. Show the leader the material and use it as a starting point for questions. The following are some questions you could ask, but let the conversation evolve so the leader gets to the issues that are important to him or her. Take good notes (to inform the discussion later), but don't feel you have to get words exactly right. Look for concepts, not specific words.

- Is this articulation of the strategy consistent with where you believe the company is going?
- If not, what's different, new, surprising, or in conflict with what you understood strategy to be?
- Do you believe executing successfully in these areas alone will get us to our goal?
- If not, what's missing?
- What specific actions are being taken within your span of control to ensure execution of any or all of these strategies?
- Which elements of strategy do you believe are at most risk of not coming to fruition and why?

- What do you believe are the biggest hurdles to effectively executing this strategy?
- Does the Conversation Platform express strategy in terms you agree with?
- Are there actions you are taking or see others taking that aren't covered by the platform?
- If not, why not?
- What is missing in the platform?
- Would you feel comfortable talking in your own words about these strategies and actions with employees?

When the interviews are done, the facilitator can then prepare a brief Situation Snapshot using material from those interviewed to illustrate agreement, confusion, and disagreement about strategy. This snapshot should not pull punches—the idea is to get difficult issues on the table. At the same time, the facilitator should protect confidentiality and keep quotes anonymous. Do not edit disagreement out of the material or soften issues to make them less

Lack of Alignment

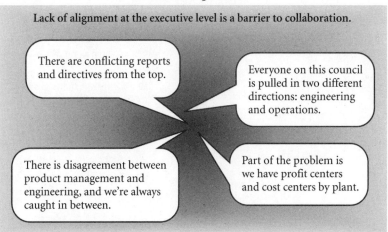

Figure 12.1.   Situation Snapshot: Identifying Alignment Issues.

contentious. The purpose of this exercise is to get issues on the table to discuss them, not to gloss over them. At the same time, make sure the material reflects where people agree as well, so the presentation doesn't overstate the alignment issues the team faces. Be careful not to attribute quotes to any specific individual or use direct quotes that identify any individual, threaten any members of the team, or reveal confidential information.

Figures 12.1 and 12.2 show examples from the Situation Snapshot that was used in the Chapter Eight dialogue session conducted for a manufacturing group. Note that the balloon "quotes" express issues in simple terms and focus on areas of conflict, confusion, and disagreement. As the facilitator presents these "quotes," he or she should confirm that these are the thoughts of the group, not those of the facilitator. This is what members of the group think, so they can't run away from it, but must deal with it in an open fashion.

This quote format is an easy way to distill and present the information. It puts the issue in simple, inescapable terms and provides support that the issue exists from the team members themselves. When the facilitator puts this kind of information up, there's nowhere to run and nowhere to hide. People have to deal with it.

Lack of Clarity Around Metrics

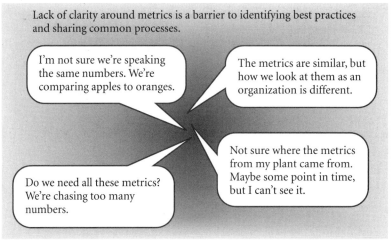

Figure 12.2.   Situation Snapshot: Identifying Metrics Issues.

THE CONSIDER-DIALOGUE-SOLVE PROCESS

We attend a lot of meetings, and many of them aren't very productive. People arrive unprepared to discuss the issues at hand, they don't listen to each other, they gloss over difficult subjects and dwell on the inconsequential, and they jump quickly to try to solve problems without really understanding them all that well. To help mitigate these kinds of problems, we've successfully used a meeting organization approach that promotes the exchange of thoughtful information, gets multiple perspectives on the table, and generates high-quality decisions. We call it consider-dialogue-solve (CDS).

The CDS framework has three components. The first is to share information well before meetings are held to discuss it. This gives people time to consider it, talk to others in their work area about their perspectives, and prepare their thinking for the discussion that is to take place. (They may not do all of this the first time you use the process, but after a few tries, they take it more seriously.) The second step, which takes place at the meeting, is to focus on discussing the information and issue without thinking about solutions. This promotes a deeper understanding of the causes behind problems and enables people to see and understand conflicting viewpoints about the issues. When teams jump too quickly to problem solving, this kind of deep understanding is lost. Finally, the third step in the CDS process (also at the meeting) is to discuss solutions and select those the group believes will be most effective.

Consider. This step gives individuals an opportunity to review and think about the subject at hand before discussing it. Provide individuals with the content to be discussed prior to the meeting—ideally a day or two in advance. This could be in the form of a meeting outline, the presentation to be discussed, or even difficult materials such as identified in the interviews discussed previously. Don't overwhelm people with documents that are too long to read, but do provide enough material so participants know what they are going to discuss and what kinds of decisions must be made. If there are conflicting viewpoints, indicate that as well. Ask each participant to set aside time to review the material and consider its implications.

Once the group gathers in the meeting, the facilitator should once again review the material and then ask the team to consider the content as a group. In this phase, the facilitator encourages participation by each of the members of the team, allowing all thoughts and concerns to be raised and documented *without conflicting discussion, but for clarification.* This helps ensure that the opinions of all the team members are put on the table for consideration. Without this no-discussion period, some team members may not be given the opportunity to express their thoughts and opinions because they get overwhelmed by the group or by forceful individuals within the group. Moreover, engaging in discussion too early often results in the team driving toward conclusions rather than simply considering the issues. As with any other session designed to share and discuss ideas, it's vitally important that all attendees participate and that everyone be given an opportunity to be heard. Stress that this portion of the meeting is *not* about debating information, options, and solutions, but rather about putting thinking and perspectives on the table for all to see and understand. Because participants are not debating each other in this phase, they are more likely to listen to each other as each person presents his or her thoughts.

Dialogue. Once each participant has had the opportunity to consider the material individually and then present his or her thinking about the material to the group, the facilitator should move into the dialogue phase of the meeting. As a group, they will now review the ideas, suggestions, and concerns that individuals raised and have a conversation about them. Focus this initial conversation on the issues themselves, *not on solutions.* By focusing on the issues without considering solutions, the group explores them more deeply and creates greater understanding. Leaders often develop new perspectives on the issues and identify additional issues that must be addressed in order to completely solve the problem. The facilitator must orchestrate the conversation, walking the group through the issues raised in an orderly fashion. For each issue, the facilitator should encourage discussion around the points of view and observations, taking the time to clarify different observations. Once the group has had an opportunity for dialogue around all the content, the facilitator can then consolidate the input into themes or specific topic matters (which will evolve from the original meeting documents provided in the premeeting materials).

Solve. The last step is to discuss solutions to the issues identified in the consideration and dialogue phases. The facilitator again should encourage discussion about alternatives, ensuring that everybody's ideas are put forth, and focusing the group on concrete actions

("What are we going to *do*?"). It's helpful to divide the solutions into three categories: (1) actions the group itself can take, (2) actions other groups need to take, and (3) issues that need to be coordinated with other groups to ensure that there is mutual support and that new actions are not working at cross purposes. This way, the leadership team can begin productive action immediately after the CDS session.

CONDUCTING A "RED FACE" TEST

We suggest conducting a "red face" test around the Conversation Platform. It's also useful in testing the effectiveness of other materials such as creative content of communication vehicles (such as posters and campaign communications).

To conduct the "red face" test, simply sit down with small groups of employees and share the Conversation Platform or other materials. The process outlined earlier in "Conducting Discussion Groups" is helpful in conducting a "red face" test. It's usually most effective to start the test with an overview of the concept of the Conversation Platform (its intention, how it can tell a story, and so on) and then to share the specific content. After the setup, the following questions will help lead a conversation to test for understanding, comfort with the strategy, and line of sight between one's job and the strategy, as well as specific language usage:

Understanding

- Based on your understanding of where the company is headed and how it's going to get there, do these points provide a good summary?

- Is this summary consistent with how most employees would view the company's direction?

- If not, what are the main differences between this summary and how most people understand the direction of the company?

- Is this disconnect caused by a difference in understanding what management has said, or is it caused by the fact that actions don't seem to match up with the words? (Explore detail.)

- If this is new to you, what do you take away from it? Does it make sense?

Line of Sight

- Now let's talk about how you see your job in these building blocks. Where would the work you and your department or function do fit in?

- Take a second and think about the priorities you have for this year and some of the actions you will take. If you had to list them under one of the building blocks, where would it go?

- If you are doing things that don't fit, is it because you are not sure how they fit into the overall strategy of the company, or because this platform doesn't do a good enough job of covering all the things we need to do?

- Do you see a lot of activity that does not fit under any of these building blocks?

Comfort

- Would you be comfortable saying these things—making the points you see in this platform with employees, if not using the actual words—to the employees you supervise or work with?

- If not, how would you want to change the building blocks? (Point out that the ideas that make up the building blocks are a lot more important than the specific words. Let them feel free to put it into their own words, but take careful note of any changes in concept.)

- How do you think employees would react to these messages of this platform if you had a discussion with them based on the summary?

- Is there anything about the language that makes you uncomfortable?

- Let's test the summary. What are some of the tough questions, or rumors, or challenges you get (or hear about third-hand) that employees bring up?

- Does the summary provide a way to address them?

- How should we change the summary to cover those items?

With the insights from these discussion groups, leaders have a good idea of whether or not the Conversation Platform will be effective deeper in the organization. If issues arise, it's best to adjust the platform to accommodate them. On Strategy communication is designed to drive action in the organization, not just to communicate what leadership would like to communicate. If that means further discussions with leadership and adjustments to the communication, so be it.

IDENTIFYING INFORMAL LEADERS

We suggest incorporating informal leaders into the People Channel in a number of ways: as people to bounce ideas off of, to provide ongoing reality checks, as part of the day-to-day communication process, and more. Identifying the informal leaders in your organization (some of whom may also be formal leaders) isn't hard. Just ask people who they are. Begin by asking yourself: Who do I go to for the inside scoop, and who do I listen to and trust—at every level of the organization? If you take some time to think about it, you can probably name many of the informal leaders yourself. Then ask some colleagues the same questions. The answers will direct you to the informal leaders. Finally, go to the people others say are the informal leaders and ask them who they go to for information (leaders tend to know who the other leaders are).

This approach usually identifies informal leaders across organizational boundaries—in a diverse set of organizational silos and geographies and across various levels. If it doesn't lead you across those boundaries, you will need to intentionally target those areas. For example, if you haven't come across an informal leader in one of your manufacturing plants, contact someone you have a relationship with there and go through the process again. Ensuring that your informal leadership ranks represent a good cross section of your population is key to its value to you.

Once you have identified the informal leadership group, select a group of about thirty that represents a cross section of the organization and create an ad hoc advisory group. You can use them as participants in the "red face" test, bounce new ideas off of them, ask for their input during strategy development and during times of change, ask their help in implementing new programs, and look to them as another set of eyes and ears to the larger organization. The group can be smaller if your organization is smaller, but we don't recommend expanding much beyond thirty because a larger group becomes difficult to engage and manage—at least at the beginning of the process. If the group grows through natural expansion—because members request participation of people they deem important to the informal communication chain—then let the group or individuals in the group assume a greater role in managing that expansion. As you align the People Channel, these informal leaders should receive special attention. Either one-on-one or as a group, explain to these informal leaders what you're asking of them. To maximize their usefulness, consider their role not only in terms of communicating to the organization but also as a channel through which you can get feedback from the organization. Also, include them in the training and support activities outlined in Chapters Nine and Ten.

SELECTING VEHICLES: OPPORTUNITIES ABOUND

There's a wide variety of communication opportunities to support local leaders in efforts to drive conversation about strategy. In fact, there are so many that selecting which ones will work the best can be a challenge. We suggest beginning with the environment in which people work (and will, in turn, have their conversations). It's better to try to adapt to the environment than to force communications into it. Walk the areas in which your managers interact, and get a feel for how you can create a presence, or just a spark. Moreover, use what's already there before creating something new (which is more work and expense). The following are some ideas with which to start.

Large and Small Office Settings

Typical office environments provide simple and effective opportunities for communication directly to employees. There are plenty of ways to get information to employees, and a variety of opportunities to spark conversations between the People Channel and employees. Some of the channels—both traditional and operating—to consider include corporate and business/functional newsletters (paper and electronic), cafeteria table tents, flyers, email, voice mail, intranet sites, posters, bulletin board postings, one-on-one conversations, direct mail, small team meetings, and large group meetings.

Remote Locations

Home-office workers, telecommuters, or people who spend a lot of time driving from location to location are often called remote workers (these days, remote can be as close as the next town or as far away as India). This is a very challenging group of people to reach, and opportunities are more limited. Certainly, leaders can send some of the vehicles used in general office settings to employee homes, including newsletters. Moreover, telecommuters rely on computers, so the intranet presents a likely opportunity for communication. For employees driving in cars, CDs can be effective. The difficulty, though, is engaging these employees in conversations. Usually, most employees have operating meetings with their supervisors on a periodic basis: weekly check-ins with supervisors, teleconferences, and the like. To influence these conversations and keep them on strategy, you should time the distribution of materials to remote employees so they receive them right before such contact points. That way, the material will be top of mind when the regular communication takes place. Also, make sure supervisors are in the loop and reminded of the information that was distributed to the remote employees reporting to them, so they are prepared to answer questions as well as raise issues outlined in the communication.

Industrial Plant Locations

The physical challenges to leadership communication in a production facility can be daunting. It's loud; employees can't necessarily talk or listen while doing their jobs; meetings are hard to hold, due to space constraints and shifts; and unions can create their own hurdles—to name just a few of the challenges. Even more so than in any other environments, supervisors are critical here. If leaders do nothing else, they should at least make sure that supervisors are prepared and equipped with the information and insight they need to have meaningful conversations with employees and answer their questions. Although supervisors are clearly the primary channel, there are creative opportunities to reach production employees, to provide On Strategy information, and to generate productive conversations, such as bulletin boards, hard-copy newsletters, posters, break room table tents, and banners.

Specific Vehicles to Leverage

There are many opportunities and needs for direct communication with employees. The specific content of the communication will determine the most appropriate vehicle to be used to get the information to the intended audience. The more significant or sensitive topics may suggest a face-to-face communication. More routine communication could be covered well in the company newsletter. And the important step of ensuring that leaders have the information first should never be overlooked.

With the proliferation of communication vehicles made possible through technology, there usually is little need to begin producing more materials. We always suggest that leaders focus on making their current vehicles more effective before considering creating new ones. That said, the following are some recommendations for making the most of current channels.

—◦◦◦—

• *Email.* We're not sure there's an individual in the corporate world who would say they don't get enough email. Nevertheless, using email for direct communication to employees can be effective in the right environment and with the right content. In many organizations, an email direct from the CEO, for example, can signal a very important message; this approach should be used sparingly to ensure that effect. Of course, you have to recognize that not all employees may have email, so you may need to use other vehicles to supplement the communication—in plant environments, for example.

• *Intranet.* Company intranets have proliferated in recent years and can be effective channels of communication. They must be simple to use, requiring users to go through no more than three or four levels to get to information they need. Because the intranet requires employees to seek out information, it's particularly important that the information provided be compelling. There has to be a reason to go there. At the same time, the intranet is a valuable place to store information that is not immediately critical to employees, but useful. This includes information about benefits, company events, and the like. In addition, it's smart to use other vehicles, such as a newsletter, to direct employees to the intranet to get more information on a particular topic. We've also seen password-protected portions of an intranet serve as a valuable resource for leadership communication tools and messages to support the People Channel. There is one pitfall with intranets that we often see: the lack of strategic ownership of the content. Individual functions seem to own pages or areas, but the IT department is often deemed owner of the entire vehicle. This structure frequently enables far too much freedom in terms of what can be posted and who's accountable for keeping it updated, quickly making the intranet a frustrating and unreliable resource. With those issues resolved, it can be a valuable channel of communication with employees.

• *Newsletters.* Most organizations have some kind of newsletter that goes to employees. Its primary focus should be On Strategy communication. Far too often, a company newsletter becomes the vehicle that is simply produced from habit, and if it disappeared no one would really notice. We worked with a client recently to redesign their employee newsletter from a content and design perspective in an effort to make it more of a strategic tool. In one discussion group, an employee asked, "Why are you trying to fix something that's not broken?" We responded with a question: "Do you get anything out of this publication that helps you do your job?" His response was, "Not really." Our point is, if your publication is not a "need to have" but at best a "nice to have," it's a missed opportunity.

• *Video.* Video can be a great vehicle, especially when you need to get a personal message out but can't logistically get everyone together. Videos can also be effective supplements to larger meetings. Many industrial plants also have video monitors in the lunch or meeting rooms, so videos can be used in that environment as well. Video should be short and either inspirational or fun (especially in operating environments).

• *Paycheck stuffers.* We include paycheck stuffers to illustrate that there are truly endless opportunities to reinforce messages with employees. Make sure you consider them all.

• *Training sessions.* When employees are engaged in training, they congregate in training rooms. You can use the physical room as a channel by putting up posters that convey an important message. As appropriate, you can also incorporate communication on strategy into the content of the training. Recognizing that the training itself should be on strategy, specific sessions can provide opportunities to share timely news and information.

• *An internal "trade show."* If there is a need to educate employees on certain topics, such as products or customers, consider setting up an internal "trade show." In a plant it might be a booth in a room accessible from the production floor, in a training room, or in the cafeteria. You can offer give-aways as an incentive for employees to visit.

• *Posters.* Posters on bulletin boards in hallways and break rooms can be a great communication tool. The message and design of the posters must catch the eye of employees and inspire conversation. Typical corporate posters quickly become wallpaper, but a departure from the norm can provide powerful conversation triggers. Make them provocative and different. And change them every few weeks— otherwise they will just blend into the environment.

• *Tent cards.* In lunchrooms and break rooms, tent cards can be easy and effective tools to communicate important messages. Coordinate them with posters to double the impact of the messaging. We worked with one client that produced a variation on the tent card idea by creating trivia cards on a particular subject they needed employees to understand in a deeper way. They put the trivia cards in metal pails on the lunch and break room tables and refreshed them on a weekly basis.

• *Production reports.* Headquarters employees and operating plants have periodic reporting documents that can be leveraged for leadership communication. These could be as simple as sheets that outline what the prior day's production was and goals for the current period. They could also be hefty documents outlining financial issues and consolidated reports. You can use a visible "corner" of these reports to reinforce leadership messages. It's also critical to ensure that the overall content of these materials is on strategy.

Generating On Strategy Conversations

We suggest walking through the physical space to see which vehicles will work best to trigger conversations. Figure 12.3 represents what we found in one industrial plant location. As you can see, the opportunities are plentiful. The same is true for other types of locations, as well. Every operation is different, though, so don't simply take our word for it. There's no substitute for the real thing—so experience it with a real visit.

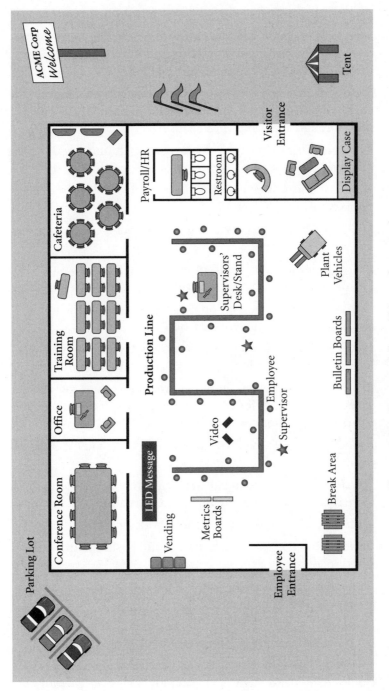

Figure 12.3. Opportunities to Trigger Conversations.

Parking Lot. Put flyers on employee windshields.

Supervisors. Supervisors walk the floor monitoring work—arm them with flyers, hats, and other triggers for conversations, as well as interesting background information.

Supervisor Station. Supervisors often have desks or stands on the plant floor. Give them posters to display and send them messages through email and voice mail.

Employees Themselves. Give employees hats, buttons, and the like to trigger conversation.

Video. Monitors often populate the plant floor—broadcast your video.

LED Signs. Plants often have rolling copy that could include your message.

Metrics Boards. Departments often track metrics on white boards; ask for some space for a small poster or written message.

Entrance. Put your message on entry signage that's often positioned at the employee entrance.

Vending or Coffee Station. Display posters, tent cards, and flyers in areas employees gather for snacks and conversations.

Break Area. Places where employees rest, lunch, and converse afford opportunities for tent cards, newsletter distributions, and informal supervisor conversations.

Bulletin Boards. Place posters, announcements, and other display communications on bulletin boards.

Vehicles. Employees often like to affix posters and decals to their forklifts, carry-alls, and other plant-floor vehicles.

Tent. Hold a "trade show" in a parking-lot tent.

Visitor Entrance. Place your materials and posters in the lobby and display case.

Rest Rooms. Advertisers have found the rest room—why not place your posters in them?

Flags and Banners. Raise your message on flagpoles that are often situated outside; put banners on the plant's facade.

Payroll or Human Resources. Paycheck stuffers not only get to employees but also might make it home! The same goes for benefits communications.

Welcome Sign. Plants often have a large roadside sign you could use to display your message to employees and community alike.

Cafeteria. The cafeteria or lunchroom is an ideal place to deliver your messages and trigger conversations. Plants often have a video display and places for posters, tent cards, newsletters, and other communications.

Training Rooms. Pepper training rooms with tent cards and posters, and ask trainers to begin their sessions with a brief conversation about your messages.

Offices. Place tent cards, provide posters, communicate through email and voicemail.

Meeting or Conference Rooms. Display posters and tent cards in conference and production meeting rooms, and also ask managers to cover your messages at the beginning of meetings.

——— Glossary of Terms

The Action Equation. *Know* + *Feel* = *Do*. The action equation first focuses a leader's thinking on what employees need to *do* in order to execute strategy or support the company's position on an issue. Then it expands that thinking to address what employees need to *know* and *feel* so they take the right actions. Moreover, it helps identify what is critical to communicate, and it filters out communication that wastes time or, worse, could be counterproductive to driving action and results.

Babble. The tendency for executives to talk about important issues in convoluted, evasive, or empty terms. Babble is seen most frequently in PowerPoint presentations filled with lists of priorities, confusing diagrams, visions and values, metrics and performance indicators, clever but empty phrases, and the catchy but irrelevant slogans promoted to build morale and fire up the troops.

Behavior Chain. A model used to understand what prevents an employee or group of employees from executing direction provided by leadership. The behavior chain is grounded in the concept that people act in a certain way for a reason, and that reason is most often driven by past experiences. The concept of the behavior chain is that one's experiences drive one's beliefs, which drive behaviors, which ultimately drive results.

Conversation Platform. Explains strategy in a very short, five-point story. The story starts with where the organization is going—which we call *the cause* because it identifies an outcome employees want to achieve. Then it articulates no more than four themes that outline how the organization will get there—what employees need to do to achieve the cause. Infused throughout is why all of it is important, to employees and the company. Because the story is told in words people actually use—rather than slogans, tag lines, or hyperbole—the conversation platform helps leaders communicate clearly and enables employees to listen and understand.

"In the moment" communication. Refers to the reality of how and when strategic direction needs to be provided to employees. With a true understanding of strategy, a leader or supervisor can answer employee questions or provide direction and strategic context in the course of everyday work—in a meeting, on the plant floor, while working through an action plan—"in the moment."

Intrinsic motivations. Those personal connections employees have to their work that gives it special meaning. These are about more than pay, recognition, or opportunity (although those things are important). They involve what people do because they *want* to do it, not just because they are *paid* to do it. A few intrinsic motivations are an affinity for customers and products, energy around the substance of the work itself, and the relationships employees have with their teams.

On Strategy. A philosophy of business communication that values simplicity and clarity. On Strategy connects business strategy to employee motivations and equips leaders from the top of an organization to the front line to communicate with employees around strategy, with the goal of driving employee understanding, motivation, and execution.

Operating communication channels. Those communication channels that are integral to the day-to-day running of the business. These are vehicles such as reporting documents, operating review meetings, functional and departmental meetings, and the other ways in which managers communicate in the course of doing their jobs.

People Channel. Leaders from the CEO to frontline supervisors make up the People Channel. The role of the People Channel is to engage employees in conversations providing direction, perspective, and information, and to pull feedback up from the ranks. In its role as the primary communication channel, the People Channel generates an active interchange of knowledge and ideas among employees and leaders, not a passive cascade of information. It uses processes and tools to engage leaders and employees in an ongoing conversation about strategy, so people have an opportunity to increase their understanding of strategy and offer their ideas and perspectives on how to improve and to better execute.

Situation Snapshot. The feedback to leadership that results following analysis of a team's alignment (or lack thereof) around strategic direction. A situation snapshot uses quotes from leadership to illustrate agreement, confusion, and disagreement on the subject of strategy.

"Traditional" communication channels. Those channels that are often mentioned when people talk about internal communication: newsletters, town hall meetings, the intranet site, and the like. These are the vehicles that tend to be managed by the communications department.

The "why nots". The reasons why people won't do what's being asked of them. These *why nots* often involve trust, confidence, commitment, or an organization's culture. They can be rooted in any number of sources, even in the long-past history of an organization.

⎯⎯ᴡᴡ⎯ **Notes**

Chapter One

1. Gallup Management Journal On-Line: Gallup Study: Engaged Employees Inspire Company Innovation. October 12, 2006.
2. M. Buckingham and C. Coffman, *First, Break All the Rules: What the World's Greatest Managers Do Differently* (New York: Simon & Schuster, 1999).
3. Survey conducted jointly by the authors and Employee Motivation & Performance Assessment, Inc., Ann Arbor, MI, 2004.
4. American Management Association survey, New York, 2003.

Chapter Three

1. L. Bossidy and R. Charan, *Execution: The Discipline of Getting Things Done* (New York: Crown Business, 2002), 69.
2. *Execution* 185.
3. L. Hawkins, "Behind GM's Slide: Bosses Misjudged Urban Tastes," *Wall Street Journal,* March 8, 2006, A1.
4. M. Dowie, "Pinto Madness," http://www.motherjones.com/news/feature/1977/09/dowie.html, September/October 1977.
5. L. Iacocca and W. Novak, *Iacocca: An Autobiography* (New York: Bantam Books, 1984), 172.
6. U.S. Chemical Safety and Hazard Investigation Board, *Investigation Report: Refinery Explosion and Fire,* Report No. 2005–04–1-TX, March 2007, 158.
7. J. Fialka, "BP's Top U.S. Pipeline Inspector Refuses to Testify," *Wall Street Journal* online, September 8, 2006.
8. Columbia Accident Investigation Board, *The CAIB Report – Volume 1: August 2003,* 199.

Chapter Four

1. C. Rosen, J. Case, and M. Staubus, *Equity: Why Employee Ownership Is Good for Business* (Boston: Harvard Business School Press, 2005).

Chapter Five

1. B. Nelson, *1001 Ways to Reward Employees* (New York: Workman Publishing, 1994).
2. F. Herzberg, B. Mausner, and B. B. Snyderman, *The Motivation to Work*, 2nd ed. (Hoboken, NJ: Wiley, 1959); F. Herzberg, "One More Time: How Do You Motivate Employees?" *Harvard Business Review*, 46 (1968): 53–62.

Chapter Seven

1. G. Miller, "The Magical Number Seven, Plus or Minus Two: Some Limits on Our Capacity for Processing Information," *The Psychological Review*, 63 (1956): 81–97.

Chapter Eight

1. R. Charan, "Home Depot's Blueprint for Culture Change," *Harvard Business Review*, Reprint R0604C (April 2006): 7.

Index

A

Action Equation (*Know* + *Feel* = *Do*):
communication on strategy in,
27–30; Conversation Platform and,
106; and conversation on strategic
direction alignment, 188–190;
defined, 221; and determination
of what employees need to do,
27–28; *Do* portion of, 27–30;
as driver of alignment, 38–39; as
driver of On Strategy content, 27;
and employees' support on issues,
29–30; and facilitated discussion, 39;
Feel portion of, 27, 31–34, 77–86;
as filter to ensure on-strategy
content, 149; *Know* portion of, 27,
30–31, 63–75; organized to promote
conversation, 36–38; overview of,
27–30; as tool to engage leadership
in strategy discussions, 121; and
"why nots," 99*tab6.1*

B

Babble: defined, 221; and employee
engagement, 9–10; negative impacts
of, 10–13
Behavior Chain, 88–92; defined, 221;
employee discussion groups and,
97, 185; and insights to address
"why nots," 88–89; list of "why nots"
revealed through, 89–91; the way it
is, 94*fig6.2*; the way you want to see
it, 95*fig6.3*
Bossidy, L., 48
BP, and nonnegotiables around safety
and maintenance, 51–53

Branding, management campaigns
related to, 155–156, 157–158
Business performance: impact of babble
on, 10–11; impact of employee
motivation on, 17
Business performance metrics:
employees' general reactions to, 125;
and leadership communication,
28–29; managers' accountability
for, 170; measuring impact of
communication on, 170–171; as
ultimate measurement tools, 169
Business plans: as communication
source, 27–28; and good leadership
direction, 47

C

Celebration campaign, and employee
decision making, 156–157
Charan, R., 48
Chief executive officer (CEO), and On
Strategy communication, 43
Coffman, C., 10
Command communication profile, and
company performance, 18
Communication: activities, in relation
to Conversation Platform, 149; and
events used to generate strategy
conversations, 153; as secondary
organizational value, 42; simplicity
and good leadership direction in,
46–47
Communication campaign: examples
of, 155–158; as extension and
intensification of On Strategy
communication, 155; identifying

priorities in, 175–176; requirements of, 155–156; research approach to performance of, 171

Communication in the moment, 186; Conversation Platform tool for, 105–108; and corporate speak, 102, 105; defined, 222; environments for, 105; and human memory capacity, 104–105; and leadership communication, 103, 186; and listening patterns, 103; preparing leaders for, 104–105; about stories rather than lists, 37–38

Communication professionals: business planning and decision making roles of, 164; competencies for, 159–161; leveraged through early involvement, 162–163; prioritizing utilization of, 164–165; as strategists and coaches, 158–159

Communication vehicles: babble as problem in, 146–147; for communication involving difficult issues, 151–152; controversial and provocative communication in, 151; coordinated with People Channel, 40–41; formal and internal, 41; and information overload due to technology, 147; and maximization of current channels, 146–148; operating channels as, 146, 148; recommendations for governing, 146; and remote locations, 197; resource guide for selection of, 148, 196–203; traditional, 146; typical office environments as, 196; used to spark conversations on strategy, 150–152; using media from popular culture, 152

Competition, employee questions concerning, 68–69

Consider-dialogue-solve (CDS) framework: challenges in, 122–123; three-step process of, 191–193; use of, 120

Conversation Platform: addressing issues over strategy, 108–114; and alignment of entire leadership group, 38–39; and babble reduction, 149; as basis of "red face" test, 123–124; communication vehicles' relation to, 149; components of, 106–107; concept chunks as summary and gateway to other information in, 108, 110*tab7.2*; connecting proof points to, 110–111*tab7.2*; and conversation on alignment around strategic direction, 188–190; defined, 221; and facilitated discussion, 39; as filter and focus, 134, 149–154; as frame for leadership's strategic message, 132; functions and use of, 105–106; management changes to, 135; as potent communication tool, 37–38; template for developing, 107–108; as tool to drive conversation on strategy, 37, 121; training for use of, 39–40, 158; value and versatility of, 114–115; vernacular language of, 113

Corporate bureaucracy, and organizational change in direction, 117

Customer decisions, employee questions on, 69–70

D

Discussion group: designing, 180–181; execution and interpretation of, 181–183; to identify motivational connections, 183–184; to inform the Behavior Chain, 185; and issues underlying poor movement of information, 172; as opposed to focus groups, 179; and "red face" test around the Conversation Platform, 193–195; as research tool, 179; use of facilitator in, 180

Do message, 45–62; and communication on strategy, 27–30; and complexity creep, 49; issues included in, 29–30; and On Strategy direction, 47–57

E

Eisenhower, Dwight, as example of leadership communication, 177

Email, as communication vehicle, 198

Emotional communication, as legitimate part of leadership communication, 82

Employee brand tour, as communication campaign, 155–156

Employee decision making, and leadership's own actions, 29

Employee emotions: and conversations connected to strategy, 22; identifying and leveraging of, 82–83; and leadership communication, 77, 82–83; and motivational connection to one's work, 16

Employee issues forum, 157

Employee motivation: business performance impact of, 16, 17; intrinsic, sources of, 31–33; and leadership's strategy around customer satisfaction, 81; quantitative formal research into, 83; and research through discussion groups, 84; triggers for, 80

Employee Motivation & Performance Assessment Inc. (EMPA) survey, 16–17; communication questions in, 171

Employee risk taking, "why nots" of, 91

Employee survey, measuring manager communication through results of, 170

Executive face-to-face program, as communication campaign, 156

F

Feel message, 27, 77–85, 86*tab5.1*; and creation of emotional connection to work, 78–79; as driver of action, 31–34; identification and leverage of, 82–83; and intrinsic motivations, 31–33; and leadership communication, 82; and leadership strategy around customer satisfaction, 81; and

motivational triggers, 79–80; and motivations not to take action, 33–34; and research on employee motivation, 83–84

Financial results, impact of communication on, 17*tab1.1*

Ford Motor Company's Pinto design, and nonnegotiable of safety, 52

Formal communication, Conversation Platform as filter for, 134

Frontline supervisors, and strategic communication, 15

G

General Motors, matrix design and leadership direction in, 48–49

Good performance requirements, leadership communication and, 19–23

H

Herzberg, F., 79

I

Iacocca, L., 52

Industrial plant locations, challenges to leadership communication in, 197

Industry layoff, preparing employees for, 157

Industry trends, company sharing of information on, 69

Informal leader networks: identifying and engaging leaders for, 126; as powerful component of People Channel, 125–126

Information flow measurement: and measure of managerial performance around communication, 172; and twelve specific attributes of flow, 172, 173*tab11.1*

Internal trade shows, as communication vehicle, 200

Interpersonal skills, leadership training for building, 40

Intranet, as communication vehicle, 198–199

Intrinsic emotions: and motivational connection to one's work, 16; and

On Strategy communication, 31–34, 79; sources of, 31–33. *See also Feel* message

Investors for the Director Accountability Foundation, 118

K

Kennedy, J. F., 53

Know message, 63–75; and employees need to know why, 64–70; as foundation for communication about strategy, 74; prioritizing employee audiences for, 64; and question of who needs to know strategy, 70–74

Kovach, K., 78–79

L

"Land of Oz" company: Action Equation and, 73*tab4.1*, 74; communication on key direction in, 57–61; motivational connections in, 84–86; and simplicity in communication, 45–46; understanding of "why nots" in, 98

Leadership alignment process, 117–127; approach to tough issues in, 187–190; choice and roles of facilitator in, 121–122; communication-driven, 119, 121; and consider-dialogue-solve (CDS) framework, 120, 122–123; and effective leadership communication, 118; identifying "why nots" in, 121–122; importance of confirming, 119; for increased collaboration across operations, 119–120; and manager's communication of leadership's message, 123–124; methods used to drive, 119; obstacles to promoting dialogue in, 123; and open discussion at multiple levels, 122–125; tendency to skip to solutions in, 122, 123; tested with line managers and supervisors, 121–122, 123, 127

Leadership communication: challenge of communicating well in, 2; and collective action, 20; in companies with large stock-owning employee populations, 68; on controversial issues, 68; and employee emotions, 77, 82–83; employee perceptions shaped by, 20; and failure to engage employees, 25–26; as foundation for employee contributions, 20; as key to motivation and action, 21; nonnegotiables in, 53–54; and performance issues, 21–23; simple and concise message in, 103, 186; style, and success or failure of People Channel, 139–140; tendency to use babble in, 9–14; as tool for company revitalization, 21–23; using lists of goals and metrics, 28–29; words-actions-words bookend approach to, 56–57. *See also* Communication in the moment; On Strategy communication

Leadership conferences, as communication campaign, 156

Leadership direction: and achievement of critical goals, 59, 60*tab3.3*; activities to support strategic actions in, 60–61; disconnect between words and actions in, 55–57; as driver of business performance, 16–19; effective, examples of, 18–19; and employees' critical decisionmaking, 50–51, 54–55; and employees' need to know why, 30–31; focused on the "What" and the "How," 49–51; nonnegotiable tenets and activities in, 51–54; physical versus abstract concept of, 50; top priorities in, 29; and tough decisions between priorities, 62

Leadership groups, informal: as ad hoc advisory groups, 195; process for identifying, 195–196; roles of, 196

Local leaders, as important communication channel, 15

M

Manager: communication metrics accountability of, 170; and leadership alignment, 121–122, 123, 127

Manager communication: and alignment with top leaders, 176; employee survey for measuring, 170; and People Channel interchanges, 36; performance, and information flow measurement, 172; in reporting leader's message to employees, 123–124

Matrix organization: complex design and mistakes in, 48–49; example of "why not" in, 90–91

Meeting organization. *See* Consider-dialogue-solve (CDS) framework

Memory game, 104; and insights on leadership communication, 186–187

Miller, G., 104

N

Nardelli, R., Home Depot change strategy of, 117–118

NASA's nonnegotiable around safety, deterioration of, 53

National Benchmark Study, 17

Newsletters, as communication vehicle, 199

Nonnegotiables: defined, 51; as integral to leadership communication and direction, 51–54

O

On Strategy communication, 145–166; applied principles of, 4; articulation of leadership's direction on, 26–27; and bottom-line results, 23–24; connected to business results through research, 170; Conversation Platform as filter for, 106, 149; defined, 222; and depth of information employees need to know, 31; determining focus of efforts in, 42; emotional (*Feel*) aspect of, 16, 31–34; focus on big goals and significant activities in, 28; forum for message promotion of, 148; framing of complex business direction in, 15; greater engagement and knowledge sharing through, 29; information sharing system for, 145; and intrinsic motivations, 31–34, 79; and *Know* portion of Action Equation, 30–31; locations and opportunities for, 200–203; long-term benefits of, 3–4; meaningful conversation in, 15–16; motivational triggers in, 79–80; overview of, 25–44; as philosophy of internal communication, 2, 23; practical strategies and tools in, 4; setting self-expectations in, 42; simplicity in, 16; three strategy steps in, 3*fig1.1*, 27, 43–44; undertaking big fixes in, 3–4. *See also* Action equation

On Strategy direction: elements of, 47–57; enabling employees' decisionmaking, 46; and identification of "critical few" strategy goals, 57–58; and nonnegotiables important to company health, 58–59; and organizational complexity, 48–49; and requirements of good direction, 46–47; simplicity and clarity in, 47–48; strategic action to pursue goals in, 59, 60*tab3.3*

One-on-one interviews, and poor movement of information, 172

Open communication: business performance and, 17; as leadership tool, 13–14

Open profile companies, performance of, 18

Operating communication channels: defined, 222; and On Strategy message promotion, 148

Operating performance, and production of quality products, 171

P

People Channel, 34–43, 131, 133; and alignment up and down the organization, 38–39; channels for keeping managers/supervisors in the loop, 136–137; and complementary leader assignments, 141–143; and contexts for information delivery, 34–35; coordinated with communication vehicles and tactics, 40–41; defined, 27, 222; and delivery of consistent strategic message to employees, 34; and expectations around communication, 41–43; expectations of top leadership in, 176; identifying and incorporating informal leaders into, 125–126, 195–196; interpersonal skill training in, 140–141; and leader conversations on strategy, 39–40; and learning opportunities, 135–136; major announcements and changes communicated through, 138–139; promotion of ongoing leadership conversation in, 139; Q&A documents provided for, 137–138; and rote cascading of information, 35–36; and support of local leaders, 135–139; traditional communication vehicles in, 35, 147–148; and updating of leaders, 135–139

Performance issues, and improvement of leadership communication, 21–23

Personnel announcement, used to reinforce desired behaviors, 149–150

Posters, as communication vehicle, 200

Product "Ride and Drive," as communication campaign, 156

Production reports, as communication vehicle, 200

R

"Red face" test: Conversation Platform and, 123, 124, 125; process in, 193–195; purpose and results of, 123–125

Reporting-and-Discussion profile, and performance problems, 18

Resource guide, 179–203; on alignment interviews and use of Situation Snapshot, 187–190; on conducting discussion groups, 179–185; for generating conversation on difficult topics, 187–190; for insights into communication and memory, 186–187

Rumor profile companies, performance of, 18

S

Senior leaders. *See* Top leadership

Senn Delaney Leadership (consulting firm), 83

Situation Snapshot: creation of, 122; defined, 222; illustrating agreement or disagreement about strategy, 189–190; quote format in, 190

Societal issues, importance of answering employee questions on, 69

Strategic communication function, 158–165; building your own capabilities for, 159; company goals as responsibility of, 162; and critical questions around decisions, 163; and staffing competencies, 159–161; tactical level in, 159, 164

Strategy: in Conversation Platform's five-point story, 37; execution, and employees' self-interests, 30; good communication's role in improvement of, 19–20; and leadership alignment, 38; ongoing organizational conversation on, 15; and true leadership alignment, 118

Strategy communication: and complementary leader assignments, 141–143; content review in, 132–133; Conversation Platform introduced into, 132–134; development of, 130; executive delivery of, 130–131; and feedback on process, 134; and knowledge of leaders beyond the top echelons, 70–71; and On Strategy training, 130–135; and practice for use of Platform, 133–134; process review in, 134; question of who needs to know in, 70–74; recognizing and strengthening weak links in, 139–141; setting expectations about responsibilities in, 131–132; support for leaders in, 135–139; tools and training for, 39–40, 129–144

Structured conversation approach. *See* Consider-dialogue-solve (CDS) framework

T

Tent card, as communication tool, 200

Time, C., 118

Top leader's role, 167–177; aggressive communication and monitoring expectations set by, 167–169; and alignment of senior teams, 118–126; and communication expectations and priorities, 175–176; and corporate bureaucracy, 117; and delegation of daily work, 169; and improvement accountability, 169–170; and leaders' focus on important metrics, 170; and leading by example, 176–177; and major communication events, 167–169; and management of strategy communication impact, 168–173; and measurement of information flow and communication effectiveness, 169–170, 172; of orchestrating communication delivery, 169; People Channel management of, 167–177; and reward or discipline for managers'

communication behavior, 174; and strategy training delivery, 130–135

Traditional communication channels, defined, 222

Training session, as communication vehicle, 148, 199

V

Video, as communication vehicle, 199

W

Wagoner, R., 48

"What do you need employees to do" question, and good leadership direction, 45–46

"Why" questions, 64–70, 74; answering, 68–70; conversations revolving around, 66; importance of leadership response to, 65–66; on issues of public concern/specific to operations, 67–68; prioritizing employee audiences for, 64; and productive dialogue between employees and management, 66; and questions beyond goals and strategy, 66–68

"Why Nots," 87–100; defined, 33, 222; examples of, 34; exploring and addressing root causes of, 92–98; and group think, 91; inaction and the blame game in, 90; involving leadership candor and motives, 89; and lack of critical due diligence, 91; and management's commitment to strategy, 89; and motivational reasons, 33; and new experience to drive new belief, 92–95; resulting from experiences and beliefs of the Behavior Chain, 88–92; and strategies for employees' work area, 89–90; research to identify, 96–98